Doing
Business
in Washington

Doing Business in Washington

*How to Win Friends
and Influence Government*

Harrison W. Fox, Jr.
Martin Schnitzer

THE FREE PRESS
A Division of Macmillan Publishing Co., Inc.
NEW YORK

Collier Macmillan Publishers
LONDON

Copyright © 1981 by THE FREE PRESS
A Division of Macmillan Publishing Co., Inc.

THE FREE PRESS
A Division of Macmillan Publishing Co., Inc.
866 Third Avenue, New York, N. Y. 10022

Collier Macmillan Canada, Ltd.

Library of Congress Catalog Card Number: 80-2313

Printed in the United States of America

printing number

1 2 3 4 5 6 7 8 9 10

Library of Congress Cataloging in Publication Data

Fox, Harrison W.
  Doing Business in Washington

  Bibliography: p.
  Includes index.
  1. Industry and state—United States.
I. Schnitzer, Martin, joint author. II. Title.
HD3616.U46F69   1981   353'.00024'658   80-2313
ISBN 0-02-910460-2

Contents

Preface

DOING BUSINESS IN WASHINGTON has not been easy through
the years. Today, Washington costs business billions of dollars
in regulatory costs, taxes, and social security payments each
year. It is almost impossible to win or even stay in the game if
you are not aware of the rules, the major actors and supporting
cast, and how best to communicate. Much of what you know
about Washington is probably superficial or a myth. We try to
dispel the myths and deepen understanding of how Washington works.

The currency of the political marketplace in Washington is
people. You must know this market to insure a profit and to
forestall bankruptcy. The personalities, backgrounds, and attitudes of these people must be understood and made a part of
any manager's plan of action. This market demands innovative
approaches and an awareness of new processes.

We feel that more American corporations should abandon
their old adversary role and adopt an advocacy strategy in their
dealings with government. Through this kind of strategy, profits can be increased, planning improved, and frustration
avoided. Increasing profits usually leads to the creation of new

jobs. This is a prime social goal of business and should be the goal of government as well. As waste and inefficiency are eliminated within the business and government framework, additional funds become available for creating jobs and other socially responsible activities. For the most part, businessmen have failed to recognize the impact of government on all phases of business operations; thus it is the goal of this book to provide a guide and models that will enhance the efficiency of managers in their relations with government.

We wish to thank lobbyists within the Sierra Club, Grocery Manufacturers of America, Food Marketing Institute, American Mining Congress, AFL-CIO, Motor Vehicle Manufacturers of America, and American Petroleum Institute; the White House, including the Eisenhower, Kennedy, Nixon, Ford, and Carter administrations; hundreds of corporations, Common Cause, and various federal departments and agencies for their time and willingness to talk about what works best in Washington for them. We were also assisted by a number of members of Congress, regulatory agency commissioners, and senior civil servants as well as their staffs. A special thank you to Congressman William C. Wampler, David C. Pruitt, administrative assistant to Congressman Jack Edwards, and Josh Bill, legislative assistant to Congressman Robert Bauman. Thanks also to Robert Wallace, our editor at The Free Press, who kept us on schedule, and Conda Boyd, who edited and typed the last draft of this book.

Doing
Business
in Washington

1

The Political Marketplace

A CBS NEWS SPECIAL CALLED "Mr. Rooney Goes to Washington" graphically illustrates the fact that the United States government, as represented by Congress, one way or another has an impact upon all businessmen. The following transcript involves a conversation between the CBS reporter, Andrew Rooney, and some businessmen who had come to Washington to obtain a part of the $95 billion in subsidies that are paid out each year by the government to special interest groups, including business (copyright © 1975 CBS Inc. All rights reserved. Originally broadcast on "Mr. Rooney Goes to Washington" on January 26, 1975, over the CBS Television Network):

> ROONEY: The United States government pays out something like $95 billion a year in subsidies. It seems as though every company and every professional organization has an office in Washington to represent its interests.
>
> Almost every bill passed in Congress influences the distribution of money, and the trick is to get more out of the government than you're putting in. Everyone knows the tax break the big oil companies get, but you don't hear much about the others. The lumber industry, for instance, gets a

1

subsidy of $130 million. The federal government pays out $244 million to fourteen shipping companies. Every American seaman is subsidized for about $12,000. And that's in addition to what the shipping company pays the sailor.

And you don't have to look to the giants of industry either to find money being handed out. We were wandering through the Rayburn Congressional Office Building one day and came on an Association of Beekeepers trying to talk Congress out of some money.

BEE CAGE PROMOTER: But without the humble honeybee, agriculture couldn't survive. There's about ninety plants in agriculture—blueberries, apples, oranges, lemons, lots of other plants—where the honeybee is completely indispensable. We have to have the services of this little animal in— again to bring the male and the female plants together.

ROONEY: Are you a beekeeper?

PROCESSOR: No. We're honey processors.

ROONEY: I see. And what is the purpose of this meeting?

PROCESSOR: The purpose is to educate the Congress on the needs of the honey people.

ROONEY: How much help from the government does the honey business get?

HONEY BUSINESSMAN: If you want me to be very candid, we don't get as much as we would like. We would like to get more help. That's one of the reasons that we're up here today.

ROONEY: What sort of help do you need from the government?

HONEY BUSINESSMAN: Well, for instance, insecticide poisoning sometimes kills our colonies. And, of course, that stops our production.

ROONEY: Are you reimbursed for that?

HONEY BUSINESSMAN: We are reimbursed for this.

ROONEY: Have you personally gotten money from the government?

HONEY BUSINESSMAN: Yes, I have, on a couple of different occasions, very small amounts.

ROONEY: And how much did you get?

HONEY BUSINESSMAN: Ah—

ROONEY: Roughly?

HONEY BUSINESSMAN: Five hundred dollars.

ROONEY: Well, he isn't the only one who got a little something. It turns out that last year alone we paid a million and a half

> dollars to beekeepers who said some of their bees had died under unfortunate circumstances.
>
> BEE CAGE PROMOTER: I'll put my hand down here, and if I jerk it back fast you'll know that I missed.
>
> ROONEY: It's all perfectly legal. You don't have to be dishonest to get rich off the government.

This conversation shows one of the ways in which government operates. Take your special interest to a legislator, an agency official, or an employee of the executive branch of government. Marshal your facts, state your case, and hope for the best. Advocacy on the part of businessmen is necessary to their survival in today's business world. The president of Republic Steel, William De Lancey, put it succinctly:

> In many ways it is correct to say that the future of the steel industry is made right here in Washington. We must regard the federal establishment as having a preeminent influence on capital investment decisions—preeminent and, unfortunately, unconstructive on many occasions. This is so because of a combination of two different aspects of federal power: in the first place, it is broad and pervasive, affecting virtually every aspect of our business, and, second, in many instances the power is being exercised to meet special and often political objectives and not to achieve goals which will bring the greatest benefit to the nation in the long run.[1]

A massive shift from market to political decision-making has occurred in American society. Increased public control of business is an ineluctable fact, for government has become an active partner in the management of the American economy; from some points of view, it is the senior partner. The role of monetary and fiscal policy in maintaining a stable, full-employment economy implies a continuous government role in a fundamental aspect of economic life. Some of the politization of economic decision-making derives from this commitment to full employment. Politization has also been increasingly introduced into the market process because a working political majority no longer sees any serious objection to using political power to change an unpopular market outcome. Group goals and group self-interest have created a state-oriented collectivist ethic that conflicts with a much more utilitarian business ethic. Government and business meet each other along a deep zone, where boundaries are poorly defined and readily changed in response to pragmatic demands.

The Changing Role of Business

A fundamental structural change that has taken place in American society is a shift from market to political decisions. More and more business decisions that affect profit or loss are being controlled and influenced by government agencies that are insulated from market pressures. The market has the virtue of including many buyers and sellers, each insistent on getting his own terms; if either is not satisfied, he can go elsewhere and seek to do better. In this way the actions of buyers and sellers have an effect on profit and loss. However, government officials and agencies are not responsive to the pressures of profit and loss, and though their decisions affect business, they have no management responsibility, nor do they have to take responsibility for their errors in judgment. In many instances, their actions exact the cost of reducing the economic efficiency of the regulated firms. For example, the regulatory process can become a labyrinth of procedural complexities that impose costs and delays on the firms. Financial resources must be devoted to dealing with government agencies. The process is often long, and the longer it takes to obtain approval for some change in business practices, the less attractive will be the change to a business firm.

Not much more than a decade ago, most business firms were largely unregulated, free to produce whatever kinds of products they pleased so long as consumers would accept them. Today, these firms are subject to detailed government regulations in almost all phases of their operations. These regulations affect most aspects of business activity. One example of this is the controversial "affirmative action" programs set in motion by the federal government, which affect business firms and unions alike. Protection of the environment is another area in which government has encroached upon the activities of most business firms. The prime example of this is the automobile industry, which now must comply with emission control standards requiring a radical reduction in the amount of hydrocarbons and carbon monoxide emitted by motor vehicles. Safety standards require automobile designers to accommodate various restraints, including air bags, seat belts, and buzzer systems, as well as specifications for brakes, safety glass, and padding of bumpers. Moreover, business expectations of profit or loss depend to some extent on policies pursued by the federal government in balancing its budget, accumulating a surplus, or running a deficit.

The Influence of Government upon Business

For the purpose of organization, government intervention in the American economy can be divided into four areas. First, there is public finance, where government is a purchaser of goods and services as well as a tax collector. Government economic stabilization policies may also be considered a part of this area. Second, government regulation and control prescribe specific conditions under which private business activity can or cannot take place. For example, government may affect the character of private business operations both directly and indirectly through antitrust and other laws. Third, government is the single largest employer in the American economy and, as such, competes directly with private industry for labor. Government also affects the level of wages and salaries. Fourth, government owns and operates business enterprises and is a major provider of credit. The impact upon business of these four areas of government intervention can be presented in some detail.

Regulation through Taxation

Government regulatin of business can be exercised through the power to levy taxes. Ever since the first revenue act of 1789, Congress has from time to time enacted tax legislation for social and economic purposes, rather than for the primary purpose of raising revenue. Taxes may be used to reward a desired performance or to penalize an unwanted performance. In certain situations it is possible that a tax may be so heavy as to suppress a business activity altogether. The Supreme Court has declared that every tax is in some way regulatory in that it interposes an economic impediment to the activity taxed as compared with others not taxed. The Court has also held that Congress may use the power to tax as a penalty or sanction in the regulation of commerce. In the Bituminous Coal Act of 1937, for example, Congress placed a tax of 19.5 percent on the market price of coal produced and sold by firms not participating in a price-fixing program. The tax was used primarily as a sanction to enforce the regulatory provisions of the act.

So great is the impact of taxes and so important are the benefits of favorable tax treatment that businesses should take maximum interest in the writing of tax legislation.

There is national concern over the decline in productivity of the American economy relative to the economies of Western Europe and Japan. One explanation for the decline in productivity lies in a low rate of business capital investments. In a twenty-five-year period up to 1973, business spending on new plants added about 3 percent a year to the nation's capital base —plants and machinery—but since then the total has risen only 1.75 percent a year.[2] Federal tax policies certainly have an impact upon investment, for tax incentives can be used to promote capital accumulation. They have been used to achieve this end in all industrial countries, particularly in West Germany and Japan. Generally, tax policies would enable companies to keep more of their earnings, either through higher depreciation allowances for the purpose of acquiring new equipment, through tax credits for the same purpose, or through lowering of the corporate income tax rate to increase retained earnings.

In addition to being a regulator of business activity, taxes provide the government with control over the nation's resources and affect the distribution of income. Both corporate and personal income taxes provide the revenues to support the welfare state, but extensive use of both, as witnessed in Great Britain, can have an adverse impact upon saving and investment. In the United States, the bipartisan Congressional Joint

Economic Committee issued a grave warning in its 1979 mid-year report: Unless major improvements are made in expanding U.S. output through increasing saving and investment in order to lift productivity, the nation will face a drastically declining standard of living in the 1980s. While Americans save little more than a nickel out of every dollar of take-home pay, the Japanese save 20 percent or more, in part because they have no well-developed system of social welfare and must provide for their old age themselves. But the rate of savings is high in West Germany, which has substantial welfare programs. Government tax policies in both countries are used to stimulate savings. In Japan, savers do not have to pay taxes on interest from deposits of up to $65,000.

There is a reverse side to the taxation coin. Government expenditures for goods and services divert resources from the private to the public sector of the economy. Government expenditures are now equivalent to almost one-third of the gross national product. There is a wide variety of spending programs that have a direct or indirect impact upon business. The federal government sponsors and encourages small business through the use of loans financed out of budget revenues. Expenditures on education by all levels of government benefit a wide variety of industries. Through its own expenditures, government has created business firms and entire industries. It has conducted much of the basic research in certain industries, and it has given impetus to technological change. The direct subsidies and indirect benefits offered business by government are too numerous to mention. Certain subsidies are designed to bring about greater production of a particular commodity than would be forthcoming if the regulation of its production were left exclusively to market forces.

Direct Government Regulation of Business

The public sector of the American economy has grown rapidly, for there has been a proliferation of new social responsibilities that various groups have asked government to assume. This can be attributed, to a considerable degree, to an ideological transformation in American society. To some extent this transformation is reflected in what has been called "interest group pluralism," which refers to the banding together of particular groups with a special or common interest. As a result of group pressure, the federal government has expanded its area of involvement in the market system. More and more government effort is being directed toward regulating areas of business conduct with which it was not previously concerned. One example of this is affirmative action. It is no longer sufficient to provide equality of opportunity to workers; instead, equality of representation for various social groups is a prime goal of federal government policy. The political process, with its goal of improving the public welfare, is exerting more and more pressure on the economic process, which emphasizes efficiency. A conflict has developed between social goals and economic efficiency.

Government regulation of business takes many forms. One important area of government regulation is antitrust activity to prevent anticompetitive business practices. This activity has sprung from the concept that such practices interfere with the efficient operation of a competitive market economy and that the most effective method of regulation is to prevent them from occurring. Then there are regulations imposed upon public utilities, which are closely regulated in terms of rates that can be charged, areas to be served, and types of services to be provided. The rates, schedules, and routes of interstate carriers are also regulated. The significance of this type of regulation lies in the fact that it is the government rather than private enterprise that controls the rates that electric power companies, interstate carriers, and other regulated industries can charge, the areas they can serve, and the services they can provide. The regulations imposed by government circumscribe the managerial alternatives open to these industries.

Then there are the areas of government social regulation of business—hiring of the handicapped, occupational safety, consumer protection, environmental protection, affirmative action, and so forth. Most of this type of regulation involves a transfer of economic resources from a large number of people to a small number of beneficiaries. For example, the Occupational Health and Safety Administration's coke oven standard protects fewer than 30,000 workers, but it is paid for by everyone who consumes a product containing steel—that is, all of us. The Vocational Rehabilitation Act of 1973 compels employers with federal contracts of over $2,500 to take affirmative action to hire handicapped workers. The oxidant standards set by the Environmental Protection Agency protect those who have respiratory problems at the expense of the general population. Mine safety regulations protect a few hundred thousand workers, also at the expense of the general public. In all of the above cases, the lobbying pressures from affected groups—steelworkers, persons with health problems, and coal miners—was substantial. Government can find it difficult to resist the temptation to do something for the benefit of some groups, even when this is accomplished at a large cost to the rest of society.

What is the optimum amount of government intervention in business and in the economy? Too much interference can lead to a stifling of individual initiative, with its emphasis on efficiency, economy, selling, and planning. Too much government carries with it the evils of centralized bureaucracy: an unresponsiveness in dealing with business and the public, the temptation of private groups to influence government policy to achieve their own selfish ends, and generally cumbersome rules of enforcement. Government frequently fails to consider whether a given problem really does need and justify public intervention. Even when action appears justified, legislators have no effective way of determining the best manner in which government help should be given. The public knows little of the trade-offs involved in government regulation—the benefits received as opposed to the cost of regulation. There is an absence of legislated incentives for regulators to use efficient means of social regulation, and no regulator is subject to the competitive forces of the marketplace. There is no punishment for mistakes made.

However, it is necessary to point out that not all rules and regulations are bad. In some cases, government had to step in because business did not respond to public demand for such measures as safer working conditions, an improved environment, and safer products. There has been a general abdication of social responsibility on the part of business—a refusal to get involved in things that didn't have a direct bearing on profits. Business also contributed to government expansion into the market system when it sought controls on costs and prices or restrictions limiting the entry of new competitors into some industries. Government regulation also became necessary because many industries came to be dominated by a few firms, instead of many firms that create the strict competitive conditions required for a pure market economy. In some cases, a single large firm or trust achieved control of a large part of the productive capacity of an industry, or a few large firms were able to act in close harmony to achieve monopolistic control of output.

Government as an Employer

One measure of the magnitude of the public sector is the number of persons employed directly by one or another governmental unit. When the armed forces are included, some 16 percent of the total labor force is employed directly by the public sector. It is likely that this percentage will increase in the future, particularly at the state and local levels of government, since the demand for social services is expected to increase. In addition, numerous other jobs are related indirectly to government employment. An army base, defense plant, or state university often supports the economy of a whole area. The public sector sets wage standards in many areas and competes against the private sector for labor resources. However, the productivity of the public sector is low in comparison to the productivity of the private sector, and as the public sector expands relative to the private sector, productivity in general declines. Unfortunately, many public-sector jobs involve make-work and provide little opportunity for creativity.

In the private sector, the profit and loss system produces an incentive to stimulate efficiency. Competition between business firms also encourages maximum efficiency in the use of capital and other resources, including labor. Both factors are lacking in government, for it is not in the business of making a profit or loss, nor is there a need to be competitive, for there is no competition between government units. There is no rationale to be productive because the stimulus is not there. No government agency has ever gone broke. In fact, some observers have argued that agency managers have strong disincentives to improve productivity if such gains lead to budget cuts. The prestige of an agency manager is often measured by the number of employees the agency has, thus the fewer the employees, the lower the prestige. The disincentive possibility means that Congress or its state equivalent must, in effect, fill the role played by the profit and loss system.

In a study on productivity in the federal government, the Joint Economic Committee of the U.S. Congress reached several conclusions. First, if overall federal productivity were increased by 10 percent, personnel costs could be reduced by more than $8 billion without a cutback in services. Resources would then be freed for use in the private sector. Second, potential savings are even greater from increasing the productivity of state and local employees. Third, there is no relation between growth in compensation and growth in productivity of federal government employees. The increase in compensation of federal employees, particularly in recent years, has been quite good. Unfortunately, it has not been accompanied by an anywhere-near-equivalent increase in worker productivity. The Postal Service, for example, has had the highest average annual increase in yearly compensation, but one of the worst productivity records. Finally, although comparisons with the private sector are difficult, available evidence suggests that productivity in the federal government sector has risen less rapidly than in the private sector.[3]

Government Ownership of Business

In the United States, all levels of government own and operate productive facilities of many kinds. Airports, but not railway terminals, are usually government-owned. Government units own and operate the plants that provide water, gas, and electricity to thousands of cities and towns, as well as local transportation systems, heating plants, warehouses, printing companies, and a wide variety of other facilities. Government produces, either directly or indirectly, all of our artificial rubber, atomic power, and many other goods. It carries on projects connected with reforestation, soil erosion, slum clearance, rural electrification, and housing. All of this does not mean that government ownership and operation is necessarily preferred to private ownership. In many cases, the resources required were too large, the risks too great, or the likelihood of profit too small to attract private enterprise, and government was compelled to perform the tasks instead.

Government credit programs are a gray area in that they do not involve outright state ownership of industry. However, federal credit programs have a direct impact on private industry that should be mentioned. Direct federal loans and loans sponsored by federally sponsored agencies have passed the $300 billion mark and continue to increase. Business is a direct beneficiary of only a small percentage of these loans; however, the sheer volume of federal loans has an impact on business through their effect on the total volume of spending in the economy and on the interest rate. Then, too, there are federal loan insurance and guarantee programs, which represent a key area of government involvement in credit markets. These programs, which in recent years have been growing much faster than direct federal loans and loans by federally sponsored agencies, constitute an extremely important instrument by which the federal government can influence the amount and allocation of credit extended in the private market. Loan insurance generates private lending in insured areas, such as housing, by reducing the risks to which private lenders are subject.

One basic issue in federal credit programs is the existence of subsidies. Many of these credit programs provide loans or insurance at rates below those that would be charged by private firms for such services, and at rates below those the government itself would have to pay to borrow money. A subsidy can be defined as the difference between the amount the borrower has to pay for a government loan and the price the borrower would have to pay for a similar loan from a competitive private lender. In essence, subsidies circumvent the forces of the free market. In the market for loanable funds, the interest rate is supposedly determined by the interaction of the supply of funds with the demand for funds. In a competitive market economy, borrowers are free to obtain loans at the going interest rate. If this market rate is 10 percent and the government charges 4 percent, then there is a subsidy that, in the final analysis, is paid by the taxpayers, including business firms. The effectiveness of the market mechanism as an allocator of loanable funds is circumvented.

There Is No Rose Garden Anymore

The public sector has grown rapidly, for there has been a proliferation of social responsibilities that various pressure groups have asked government to assume. As a result, the federal government has extended its involvement in the market system. More and more government effort is being directed toward cushioning individual risks and regulating personal and institutional conduct. The cumulative impact of its actions impinges heavily upon business. In some cases, this was necessary because business was not responsive to public demands for such measures as safer working conditions; in other cases, actions occurred because business is a visible symbol for discontent on the part of special interest groups. Conflict developed between a political system that placed emphasis on public well-being and economic equality, and business, which has adhered to a utilitarian ethic of efficiency. There has been a conflict between social goals and efficiency, and social action to benefit a few groups has resulted in interference with efficiency in the market to the detriment of society as a whole. Moreover, government regulation is not cheap, nor is there any guarantee that social goals will be accomplished by it.

Business firms must be well aware of the economic and social implications involved in government legislation and regulation if they hope to function successfully within a changing society. Old ideas and assumptions are slipping away in the face of a changing reality and are being replaced by different ideas and assumptions, which are often contradictory. The role of the state has changed drastically, and its impact upon business is great, not only in terms of cost but in terms of restructuring the entire operational activities of business. It is necessary to illustrate how government regulation impacts upon business not only in terms of money and real costs, but upon the organizational structure of business as well. Management no longer has the latitude in which to manage that it once had.

2

The Cost of
Regulation

SENATOR LLOYD BENTSEN OF TEXAS has made the statement
that "federal regulation has become America's number-one
growth industry," adding, "We write one page of law and we
get fifty pages of regulation." [1] He is right on both counts.
Take, for example, the cost of cleaning up the environment.
Environmental safeguards were enshrined in federal law only
after years of struggle between proponents of protection and
recalcitrant industrialists who predicted economic disaster if
they were forced to comply. By the early 1970s, Washington
took it for granted that cleaning up the environment was a goal
that had to be met. The cost of regulation to the consumer—to
the extent that it was considered at all—was thought to be
benign, for there was the assumption among environmentalists
that polluters would pay for the cleanup out of their own pock-
ets. However, business after-tax profits are not nearly large
enough to cover the myriad of mandated regulatory costs that
come out of Washington, and to a businessman, if he expects
to stay in business long, any expense will be largely or entirely
passed through to consumers in the form of higher prices.

A Washington University study commissioned by the Sub-

committee on Economic Growth and Stabilization concluded
that federal government rules and regulations in 1979 would
cost the American people $102.7 billion—$4.8 billion in administrative costs of the regulating agencies and $97.9 billion in
compliance costs by the private sector of the U.S. economy.[2]
The cost of this regulation is felt in the prices of virtually all
products purchased by consumers—costs which, for example,
have increased the price of a new automobile by an average of
$700 during the 1970s. A considerable part of the cost of reg-
ulation is borne by small business firms, which supply 55 percent of the employment and 50 percent of the gross national
product of the United States. It is more difficult for small firms
to afford the cost of regulatory compliance, and the owners,
unless they are speed readers, do not have the time to read the
70,000 pages published annually in the *Federal Register* to keep
abreast of new and changing regulations. Thus, it is conceivable
that excessive government regulations, including the cost of
paperwork compliance, could result in making the individual
entrepreneur an endangered species.

Problems of Social Regulation

Few people would argue for complete elimination of all
forms of government regulation. The objection is to a rather
willy-nilly and often capricious application of regulations.
Many enforcement agencies have confused priorities, set
sweeping standards on the basis of questionable evidence, and
thus have imposed enormous and unnecessary costs upon businesses and consumers. For example, the Department of Transportation has attempted to require air bags in all cars as a way
to increase passenger safety. It is estimated that the installation
of the air bags will add $500 to the cost of every new car—yet
no research has demonstrated that they are more effective than
seat belts, which cost only $50. The Food and Drug Adminis-
tration's proposal to ban saccharin, currently delayed by Congress, is another example of questionable evidence and
unnecessary cost. Saccharin had caused cancer when fed in
huge dosages to laboratory rats, but no harm to human beings

had ever been demonstrated; even so, the FDA wants saccharin eliminated from the American diet, at an estimated cost to food companies of $110 million a year.

The single most important problem that pervades government social regulation is the absence of any mechanism to compel the regulators to examine the economic trade-offs among different ways of achieving a given regulatory goal. Since few citizens can possibly know how much alternative policies will cost them in terms of reduced resources for buying food, shelter, or medical care, the decision to minimize the economic cost of social regulation is seldom the one that appears politically most prudent to administrators of regulatory agencies such as the Occupational Safety and Health Administration and the Environmental Protection Agency. They often end up choosing a needlessly expensive regulation or a very tight standard that could not be justified by its benefits and costs, for their principal goals are to improve environmental quality or human health and safety at minimum political cost, not necessarily at the lowest economic or social cost. They do not expend their own budgetary allotments when they require outlays by private firms on pollution control or safety devices.

Social regulation, unlike traditional rate-setting regulation for public utilities, is not subject to market forces and public opinion that can limit costs. The public reaction to rising utility rates, for example, has been an important constraint on public utility commissions. The disparity between intrastate and interstate airline tariffs increased the pressure for deregulation of interstate airlines. Because the price of such regulation is visible, it invites a political response. Moreover, when prices are set above the cost of production, many customers will shop for alternative sources of supply. Thus the Interstate Commerce Commission's decision to allow value-of-service pricing for interstate trucking and generally to allow interstate truck rates to exceed the cost of service has led shippers to find alternative, unregulated forms of transportation. Similarly, improperly set toll rates have induced large users of communications to establish their own microwave systems or to increase them from non-Bell carriers.

The corrective forces of the market and public opinion do

not exist in most areas of social regulation. A businessman has no alternative but to comply with a mandatory standard if the regulatory agency has sufficient enforcement tools. The cost of health, safety, and environmental standards is not directly observable; therefore, the public cannot separate the mandatory costs from other costs incurred in producing a pound of aluminum or a ton of paper. Social regulation often involves some aspect of human health or safety that can be used by a regulatory agency to invoke strong emotional support for its actions, no matter how extreme or costly they may be. After all, who could be so callous as to be opposed to protecting workers from exposure to a cancer-producing agent? What all of this means is that much social regulation cannot be subject to rational analysis, no matter whether it is costly and inefficient. Social regulation is potentially very costly, particularly if regulators are unchecked in their zeal to require expenditures by producers or consumers.

Costs of Regulation to Business

The cost of government regulation to business can take several forms. There is the paperwork cost of filling out a wide variety of government forms. Another type of cost involves capital outlays for such items as pollution control devices and health and safety equipment. Then there are costs associated with government procurement contracts with private business firms. Often these contracts, which are frequently used to achieve various economic and social objectives, are let at costs well above those that would prevail under competitive market conditions. The Davis-Bacon Act, for example, tends to increase the cost of private construction projects through government stipulation of wage rates higher than those that would prevail if the market were allowed to function competitively. Federal laws also increase the cost of hiring and promoting the work force. An example is government-mandated fringe benefits, such as social security, which are costs that have to be paid by the employer. Finally, the cost of government regulation has to be examined in terms of impact on the operational structure of most business firms.

Paperwork Costs

The Commission on Federal Paperwork was created by Congress to assess and find ways to reduce government-mandated paperwork. The commission estimated that private industry spends between $25 billion and $32 billion annually on completing and filing federal reports.[3] Of these costs, approximately $15 billion is absorbed by the small business sector. There are over 4,400 different federal forms that the private sector must fill out each year, which takes an estimated 143 million man-hours. State and local governments also have their paperwork requirements, which place an additional cost on business. Paperwork is often wasteful and duplicative, and its cost falls disproportionately upon small business firms. The Manufacturing Census forms arrive at about the same time small business owners are deeply involved in preparing their annual income tax returns. Large companies are also affected by the cost of paperwork. Dow Chemical, in a study made to identify and quantify federal regulatory costs incurred annually, estimated its federal paperwork costs to be more than $20 million.[4]

Paperwork for all levels of government places an unproductive burden on business firms, for time has to be diverted to filling out questionnaires and replying to orders and directives. In addition, time may have to be spent in court appeals concerning rulings and regulations. The smaller the business, the greater the amount of entrepreneurial time has to be spent in filling out government forms. If entrepreneurs don't do it themselves, their employees' time has to be diverted to filling out the forms. Filling them out may require more educated and more expensive workers than those normally assigned to producing the company's products. Then, of course, time has to be spent in keeping track of changes in the forms. Little thought has been given by government to the desirability of minimizing unnecessary data and reports until very recently, when many complaints by business firms were received by Congress.

Production Costs

Although the paperwork burden may be one of the most bothersome elements attached to federal controls over business, other aspects of regulation can be far more costly. Take, for example, compliance with the environmental laws. Improvement of the quality of the environment will be expensive so far as business and society are concerned. The U.S. Council on Environmental Quality estimated that the private sector's capital investment requirements for pollution control equipment would come to $112 billion in the decade 1972–1981.[5] This estimate was made in 1973; the actual amount is around $200 billion. Compliance with pollution control equipment standards can be translated into higher industrial production costs. Federally mandated pollution control costs have had an impact on the automobile industry and have contributed to an increase in the price of motor vehicles. Emission control standards cost Chrysler $620 per car in comparison to a cost of $340 per car for General Motors, illustrating that GM can spread costs over a larger number of cars sold.[6]

There is also the problem of opportunity cost, which is defined as the value of the benefit that is foregone as a result of choosing one alternative rather than another. This is an important concept, because the real cost of any activity is measured by its opportunity cost, not by its outlay cost. Thus, if resources are used to control pollution, society gives up all the other goods and services that would have been obtainable from those resources. If resources were not scarce, there would be no opportunity cost. But resources are scarce, and they have alternative uses. So, for example, resources devoted to the manufacture of pollution control equipment might have been used to manufacture houses instead. Put in a strictly environmental context, opportunity cost means that water, when allocated to a recreational use, carries the cost of sacrificing other activities that also require water use. Whether it should be so used, therefore, depends not only on whether the intended use is good, but whether it is better than the use to which the resource could otherwise be put.

Environmental and other areas of social regulation add to production costs in a number of ways. In the area of occupational safety, for example, planned industrial investment in health and safety equipment was estimated to be $3.4 billion in 1977.[7] The Occupational Safety and Health Administration (OSHA) has estimated that it will cost American industry an aggregate of $13.5 billion to bring existing facilities into line with existing OSHA noise standards. In the consumer area, government is clearly in the process of becoming the protector and confidant of the consumer. Laws have been passed with which business firms have to contend as a cost of operation. Take, for example, the federally mandated automobile safety features that have been imposed on the automobile industry. Seat and shoulder belt requirements added, on the average, $11.51 to the price of a new car.[8] In the 1974-model year, the interlock system and other changes required to meet federal safety standards added an additional $107.60 to the price of a new automobile.[9] Since consumers have unequal tastes for safety, there is a need to recognize trade-offs between safety and other criteria important to consumers.

Government regulation also adds to total production costs by raising personnel costs. Fringe benefits, which add to the cost of labor, are a major example of regulation leading to higher production costs. Employers are also affected by laws concerning the recruitment and testing of employees. The impact of affirmative action upon an employer's cost can be considerable. The sheer volume of resources required to gather and process data, formulate policies, make huge reports, and conduct interminable communications with a variety of federal officials is a large, direct, and unavoidable cost to any employer—whether or not the employer is guilty of anything, and whether or not any legal sanction is ever imposed. Employers also want to avoid lawsuits that involve the payment of restitution to employees who charge that discrimination has deprived them of past promotions and raises. Hiring workers has become slower, more laborious, more costly, and less certain. It is not that it costs more to hire women and minorities, but that it becomes more costly to hire anyone.

International Costs

In a recent issue of *Business Week,* there was a feature article called "The Decline of U.S. Power." [10] This decline is both economic and political. In the economic area, the decline is reflected in decreasing productivity relative to other countries. Over the last ten years, nonfarm private productivity increased only 10 percent—the same as in Britain, but less than half as much as in France and West Germany, and less than a quarter as much as in Japan. In 1950 it took seven Japanese or three German workers to match the industrial output of one American; today, two Japanese and about 1.3 Germans do as well.[11] This decline in productivity can be attributed to a number of factors—some tangible and others not so tangible. One tangible factor is the increase in size of the public sector. It is harder to increase the productivity of a bureaucrat than an assembly line worker.

Certainly a contributing factor to the decline in U.S. productivity relative to other industrial nations is excessive government regulations. Government rules have forced companies to spend cash on costly environmental, health, and safety equipment rather than on modern machines. The Joint Economic Committee of the U.S. Congress deplored the fact that U.S. industry in 1977 had to spend $6.9 billion for pollution control equipment that did not contribute directly to the production of measured output.[12] But that is not the main point, which is that in the arena of international competition, foreign competitors play by a different set of rules. Take, for example, Japan. There has been a close working relationship between business and government in Japan that dates back to the Meiji Restoration.[13] The Japanese government wants its multinationals to succeed in international competition and promotes business interests by means of special financial privileges, subsidies, low interest rates, and tax policies designed to promote investment and corporate savings.[14]

These different sets of rules by which foreign competitors play involve antitrust laws, antibribery and antiboycott laws, and more lenient environmental laws. U.S. antitrust law is based on the principle that competition per se is good.[15] The Western European and Japanese governments do not take a similar position, particularly with respect to foreign trade.[16] Industrial concentration and anticompetitive agreements are regarded as beneficial, so long as they lead to increased productivity, economic growth, and the advance of technology. The West Germans, Japanese, French, and other multinationals are not bothered by antibribery and antiboycott laws. The U.S. Foreign Corrupt Practices Act makes it a criminal offense for any corporation, its employees, or agents to make improper payments to foreigners to win business contracts or influence foreign legislation. Critics argue that this law makes it difficult, if not impossible, for U.S. companies to do business in parts of the world where bribery is accepted as a way of life. To a greater degree than most of their foreign competitors, U.S. companies are also subject to a variety of human rights and environmental constraints on exports and foreign investment.

The most important development in recent years has been the rise of the foreign multinational corporation. Japanese and European multinationals have expanded aggressively into such traditional U.S. corporate preserves as South America and Mexico. United States dominance of certain world markets has declined sharply. In 1953 the United States was responsible for 70 percent of the world's production of automobiles; by 1978 its share had declined to 30 percent. The once-dominant position of the United States in the production or construction of television sets, cargo ships, synthetic fibers, plastics, and steel has passed to European and Japanese firms. Total sales of the overseas affiliates of foreign multinationals have now passed those of U.S. subsidiaries abroad. Their direct investment abroad has also caught up to the U.S. level, and may have passed it. Moreover, the United States has become an attractive place in which to invest, as more and more European and Japanese multinationals are finding out. The world marketplace has drastically changed since France's Jacques Servan-

Schreiber wrote a book called *The American Challenge,* in which he warned of an American takeover of European industry.[17] Today, it may be the other way around, as foreign firms are acquiring American firms in increasing numbers.

Foreign multinationals receive more support from their governments in the arena of international competition than do American firms. The U.S. government, according to many American executives, has no effective policy for supporting American business firms abroad. This lack of a supportive relationship causes a loss of business to European and Japanese firms, whose governments apparently want them to succeed in world competition. Although the complaints of American executives may be overstated, there is no question that there is a closer working relationship between business and government in, say, Japan than in the United States. The U.S. Export-Import Bank does not compete with many foreign government banks in terms of speed, simplicity, or cost. The tax systems of other countries, particularly when applied to international business, are more favorable than the system of the United States. Foreign diplomats work much more closely with their home multinationals than do the diplomats at our embassies.[18] This difference in government attitudes can lose sales and contracts for U.S. firms.

3

The Second Managerial Revolution

PROMINENT BUSINESS ECONOMIST Murray Weidenbaum has made reference to what he calls "the second managerial revolution."[1] The first was noted by Adolfe Berle and Gardiner Means more than four decades ago.[2] These observers of the American corporate scene were referring to the divorce of the formal ownership of the modern corporation from the actual management. In the last century, the new aristocracy of the country was made up of wealthy entrepreneurs and businessmen. Their prototypes were such men as John D. Rockefeller and Andrew Carnegie. They were the epitome of the Protestant work ethic, successful in a competitive race where victory went to the swift and resourceful, and they were supported by a philosophy that helped to explain and justify their preeminent position—the philosophy of social Darwinism. To put it simply, social Darwinism was Darwin's biological theory of "survival of the fittest" applied to the business world.[3] Social Darwinists opposed government intervention in the operation of the economy.

The corporation form of business eventually superseded the Carnegies, Fords, and Rockefellers of the world and became

25

the dominant business unit by the end of the last century. One advantage of the corporation was that it was better able to facilitate large-scale production. It was also easier to raise capital through the sale of stocks and bonds. But the sale of stock made its purchaser an owner of the corporation, and there developed the divorce of the formal ownership of the modern corporation from the actual management. In the corporate system, the owner of industrial wealth eventually was left with a mere symbol of ownership, while the power, responsibility, and substance that had been an integral part of ownership in the corporate beginning were transferred to a separate managerial group into whose hands control fell. In other words, Standard Oil was no longer owned and run by the Rockefellers; to the contrary, it was operated by a managerial class, completing the separation of ownership and management.

The second managerial revolution, according to Weidenbaum, is now under way—a silent bureaucratic revolution in which the locus of the decision-making process of the American corporation is shifting once again, this time to Washington. The shift is from the professional manager selected by the corporation's board of directors to a vast cadre of government regulators, selected willy-nilly, who influence and often control the key decisions of the typical business firm. There is a considerable element of truth in what Weidenbaum is saying. Government has taken on unprecedented tasks of coordination, priority setting, and planning in the largest sense. Government has become big in the United States—probably bigger in proportion to our population than even in those countries we call "socialistic." It is difficult for managers, especially those in large corporations, to operate in an environment in which old ideas no longer seem to work and new ideas, particularly those of government, are poorly defined.

Government influence and control over the business decision-making process can take several forms. For example, there are government controls over the internal operating procedures of private companies. Employers are subject to laws governing minimum wages, overtime hours, equal pay, equal employment opportunity, and relations with unions. Each department of the typical industrial corporation has its counterpart in a federal agency that controls or strongly influences its internal decision-making. The finance department must keep its books and records so as to satisfy the Internal Revenue Service and the Securities and Exchange Commission. The research and development department must work on products and processes that meet the requirements of the Environmental Protection Agency, and the personnel department must gear its hiring policies to the edicts of the Equal Employment Opportunity Commission.

Impact of Regulation on Management

Government regulation of business has had an impact upon the top management of all corporations. No longer can management afford to be indifferent to what is going on in Washington. The approach "If you ignore a problem long enough, it will go away," does not work, for Washington is here to stay. Management must be aware of what is going on in Washington, for that is where the laws are made that have a direct impact upon business. Since government is taking on a much larger and more pervasive role in the economy than has been traditional in the past, management must take a much more active role in areas that directly impinge upon business. Nothing can be accomplished by damning the federal government at Rotary Club luncheons.

Management must now accept responsibility for the internal monitoring of company operations, including the hiring and promotion of personnel, personnel safety, product evaluation, and other areas. It is subject to liabilities and restrictions. For example, management has to assume responsibility for product safety. It can be held liable for product safety and pure food and drug standards. Proof of wrongdoing is no longer needed, for liability is assumed for injuries to the consumer when the results of such injury are reasonably foreseeable, regardless of whether the product is itself dangerous or harmful. A consumer need not prove that a manufacturer was guilty of negligence.

Management also has to be responsible for both internal and

external communication. More emphasis must be placed on government relations and political involvement. It is more desirable today for managers, who are spokesmen for the companies they represent, to possesss some degree of charisma and speaking ability. There is a need to improve the managerial image. The former president of General Motors, Charles Wilson, once made the statement, "What's good for General Motors is good for the country." As spokesman for the largest corporation in the world, his statement hardly did the image of business any good, even during the tranquil Eisenhower period. The inability of business to clearly articulate its positions has contributed to a generally negative attitude toward business on the part of the public.

Impact of Regulation on Company Operations

Until rather recently, most American business firms were largely unregulated and free from public accountability by legislation or by court action rather than by voluntary initiative. About the only thing the typical business firm had to worry about, as far as government was concerned, were minimum wage laws. A business was free to produce what it wanted, subject to few constraints. In the case of the automobile industry, it too was free to produce the kinds of cars it pleased, subject to consumer acceptance. Pricing policies were geared to provide a high rate of return on capital, based on a standard volume concept. The automobile was regarded as the shining example of capitalist enterprise, and marketing practices were geared to get the product from producer to consumer as quickly and efficiently as possible. The future looked good, for the automobile was a status symbol and a means of mobility and freedom to each American family.

How everything has changed within a short period of time! Today, automobile and other companies are subject to detailed government regulations that cover all phases of operations, from production to distribution. The automobile industry is subject to a number of different regulatory constraints, including product safety, noise, emission of pollutants, and fuel economy. At times, even pricing policies are in response to guidelines laid down in Washington. To some degree, this regulation is the fault of the automobile industry, which failed to recognize social changes. However, there was a certain amount of regulatory overkill on the part of the federal government in response to pressures exerted by consumer and environmental groups. Anyway, the experience, as far as the automobile industry is concerned, has not been good, and Chrysler has blamed its current financial predicament in part on an excess of government regulation.

Impact upon Production

Government regulation has changed the process of production. For one thing, an increased share of investment is not productive. When capital expenditures on pollution abatement are compared to total capital expenditures on new plants and equipment, it is estimated that about eight cents out of every investment dollar goes for pollution abatement. Estimates indicate that the petroleum industry devotes around 15 percent of its total capital outlays to pollution control equipment.[4] This investment is a dead weight loss in the sense that it provides no return. Moreover, alternative investments that could provide a rate of return have to be foregone. It is incorrect to relate the cost of an activity or a decision to what a business is doing. It is what the business is not doing, but could be doing, that is the correct cost consideration.

For some industries, compliance with environmental regulation means a good deal more than simply buying a few pieces of pollution abatement equipment; it means a fundamental restructuring of markets, products, and basic economics. Coal producers, for example, can face problems of redistributing, possibly under federal statutory direction, their clean coal to the most polluted areas of the United States, thus abrogating or upsetting a number of existing contractual relations. Coal producers have had to find ways of developing low-sulphur deposits. The costs of opening these deposits to meet the growing demand for coal are substantial. Coal producers also have had to cope with new processes to perfect coal cleaning, gasifi-

cation, and liquefaction. If they are successful with these processes, they will be selling to either entirely new or to sharply
constricted markets; either way, they will have to shoulder huge
investment and cash-flow burdens.

There are other areas where government regulations impact
upon production. Employer responsibility for employee safety
has created the need to redesign plants. Noise abatement standards have created limits on noise emissions from many products, as necessary to protect the public health, safety, and
welfare. There is a need to expand quality-control functions to
avoid, for example, time-consuming product recalls. It has also
become necessary to devote more time to quality-control standards, given more stringent consumer product safety laws. The
Consumer Product Safety Act, for example, requires manufacturers to conduct a testing program to assure that their products will conform to the established safety standards. The manufacturer is held accountable for knowing all safety criteria
applicable to their products, and requires that safety standards
be described in detail. Finally, research and development must
involve processes and products that conform to environmental
and safety laws.

Impact upon Marketing

Distribution must now be geared to accepting the possibility
of product recalls. The Consumer Product Safety Act requires
a manufacturer to take corrective action when a product contains a defect that could create a substantial product hazard.[5]
This can result in product recall, which involves distribution in
reverse. It is necessary to reduce the cost of recalls, which can
be done through improved record-keeping and the use of com-
puters. Regulation also has an impact on labeling and advertising. Product labels must be more informative, and advertising
has to shift the purpose of product packaging and labeling
from sales promotion to safety and efficiency information.
Warranty standards are affected by the Consumer Product
Warranty Act of 1975.[6] Warranties must be easy to understand.
A written warranty can be created by point-of-sale advertising
or by other means of advertising if the affirmation is in writing.

Companies must label warranties as either "full" or "limited" and must provide a statement as to the work that will be done, at whose expense, and the period of time a warranty will last. The act has particular significance to business firms in the area of marketing in terms of product information.

Impact upon Employment Practices

In recent years the focus and emphasis of government regulation has been directed toward social goals. One example of this new form of regulation involves the employment of women and members of minority groups, or as it is commonly called, affirmative action. A business firm now has to redesign itself according to certain overall criteria. Noncompliance with government orders can lead to severe penalties. For one thing, there is the probable loss of federal contracts, upon which many business firms depend. Employers also want to avoid lawsuits that involve the payment of restitution to employees who charge that discrimination has deprived them of past promotions and raises.[7] Moreover, a fundamental question raised by affirmative action is whether American society wants equality of opportunity or equality of result. The latter involves a numbers game in which there is supposed to be representation at all levels of a firm on the basis of ascriptive qualifications—race, sex, national origin, and so forth. The issue of equality of opportunity or equality of result is fundamental to business operations.[8] What value does individual merit have in a business organization, and what value do collective group rights have?

Affirmative action is only a part of the total employment picture. Employers are also affected by laws concerning the recruitment and testing of employees.[9] In the area of advertising for workers, it is unlawful for an employer to print or publish an advertisement relating to employment that expresses a preference based on sex, except where sex is a bona fide occupational qualification for employment. Somewhat similar requirements are applied to application forms with respect to race, age, and marital status. Courts have held that inquiries into a prospective employee's criminal record would be racially discriminatory unless the inquiry and the answer it was designed to elicit were somehow directly related to the total assessment of the employee. The same is true of all other types of preemployment testing and standards, such as aptitude tests, IQ tests, and educational achievements. It does not matter that there is no intent to discriminate. If the effect is discriminatory, it will be disallowed.

International Operations

Since many American corporations are multinational in their operations, government regulation can be a key factor in determining their success or lack of it. Competition from European and Japanese multinationals—backed, financed, and often wholly or partly owned by their home governments—has become fierce. Almost unanimously, executives of U.S. multinational corporations regard Washington's regulatory maze and a general indifference to their interests abroad as factors working against their success in international competition. Across the board, from government-to-government trade deals, to export financing, to antitrust laws and other government regulations, foreign multinationals enjoy the luxury of complete government backing. A published study by an antitrust task force of the U.S. Chamber of Commerce concluded that American exporters and overseas contractors are restricted by U.S. antitrust laws in comparison to foreign firms.[10] Most foreign firms are provided with better export financing than American firms, and most are provided various forms of tax relief. American business firms feel they have lost business to foreign competitors because the latter have been able to form consortiums and offer package deals, while American firms have had to bid independently.

A Need for Business Involvement

It is a characteristic American response to a perceived wrong to pass a law and punish the culprit. We have not only regulated business, but morals as well—the most comprehensive experiment being the 1919–1933 experience with prohibition of the use of liquor. The degree of regulation of business life in the United States is awesome in its range and scope. Probably not one area of business activity today is unaffected by some kind of regulation imposed by a myriad of government agencies that have the power to govern the behavior of regulated firms. Louis Jaffe, of the Harvard Law School, has stated the situation most accurately: "Federal agencies are not so much industry-oriented or consumer-oriented as regulation-oriented. They are in the business of regulation, and regulate they will, with or without a rationale." [11] But business interests, at least until recently, have often been diffused and poorly organized, and have come off second or third best to interest groups that are more vocal and better organized. Today, everybody organizes and goes to Washington to fight for something.

Critics of American corporations are most vocal in their criticisms. Ralph Nader, self-appointed knight exemplar and number-one professional critic of American business, catalogs a number of corporate sins—business crime, concentration of wealth and income, undue reliance on technology, unsafe products, economic concentration, undesirable conduct of multinational corporations, and so forth.[12] American corporations are compared by Nader to carnivorous dinosaurs of prehistoric times—*Tyrannosaurus rexes* that prey upon society.[13] The corporate satans have to be exorcized by increased government control over business—the Nader prescription for all problems. Legal mechanisms would be created by which groups affected by corporate decisions—workers, consumers, suppliers, residents of neighboring towns and cities, and the general public—would be somehow represented in decision-making. Corporations would be required to make public disclosure of such matters as hiring policy (for example, the number of blacks, women, and Chicanos employed), occupational health data, cost data, information on activities causing pollution, market share data, line of business data, and much more.

The vaunted power of corporations relative to other American institutions appears to be overrated. For many years, organized labor has enjoyed much more clout in government than business. Big government itself exercises more power than corporations. When business has succeeded in altering government legislation, it has usually been done in conjunction with other groups, notably organized labor. A good example involves amending the Clean Air Act of 1970.[14] Both business and labor opposed an amendment which would have required more stringent emission standards for automobiles. The opposition of business alone would have been insufficient; organized labor had more clout with Congress. In fact, the political victories of business are usually temporary defeats of antibusiness legislation. Business rarely makes a legislative proposal without substantial support from groups like labor, as in the case of the Lockheed and Chrysler loans.

Business now realizes that its political position is that of a minority, and that other institutions, especially unions, can exert superior political influence. However, it has yet to identify itself firmly with broad public-interest movements. An important priority of business is to create a more viable relationship with government instead of confronting government in an adversary relationship in which each institution meets along a deep zone, where boundaries are poorly defined and border warfare is always prevalent. Business may not love government and vice versa, and there can never be the close corporation that exists between business and government in Japan, but there is room for more cooperation and perhaps peaceful coexistence. Therefore, the remainder of this book is designed to show the best ways of getting involved in the political process—from the making of laws by politicians to their implementation by regulatory agencies. But first there is the need for improved public understanding of the role of business. There is a general absence of political competence within most business organizations that results in an inability to attract public support for issues affecting the interest of business.

Corporate leaders are increasingly seeing their jobs as quasi-public. Irving S. Shapiro, chairman and chief executive officer of E. I. duPont de Nemours and Co., notes that "in recent years, there has been a fundamental change in the approach taken by many chief executive officers. They have become personally involved in the governmental process. Because of the increasing impact of government actions on business operations, this is just as important as being skilled in knowing how to manufacture a product or administer a payroll." [15] Thus management complexity has increased, and political management has assumed a larger role in determining "the legitimacy and viability of the firm in society." [16]

4

Business as Advocate

EFFECTIVE COLLABORATION BETWEEN government and business is a sine qua non for dealing with most of the major problems facing American society today. Many unresolved issues are a consequence of the failure of business and government, the two primary institutions in American society, to function effectively, both individually and in relation to each other. At best the relationship between business and government is comparable to the joke about how porcupines make love—very carefully; at worst the relationship has been tantamount to border warfare. But societies survive because crises that need to be resolved are eventually resolved and, with luck, the forces making for social maturity will overbalance the forces making for disintegration. The business-government relationship can improve because by nature business firms are adaptable, for they have to be in order to survive. In adapting, they may have to alter the utilitarian ethic—but perhaps not by much. Then, too, business firms may acquire a political constituency or, more likely, have constituencies thrust upon them, as government becomes more and more the focal point for private grievances.

36

Improving Relations with the Public

Barriers continue to exist between business and government and the public. In part, this is the fault of business, for it has maintained a stance of aloofness that inhibits cooperation with government on national policy problems. It is necessary, however, to improve its image with the public to broaden its constituency. Business is generally held in low esteem by the public. This low esteem is not new, for big business has been consistently unpopular over the years. The animus began in the last century, when the large corporation first began to displace small shopkeepers and artisans, and then grew stronger during the period of robber baron exploitation and labor wars. More of this animus was directed toward individuals—Rockefeller, Vanderbilt—than business itself.[1] The development of the trust redirected some of the public's discontent toward the impersonal big business. During the 1920s, business improved its public image considerably, not so much through its own efforts but because the time was one of unprecedented prosperity. However, the economic collapse of the 1930s had an adverse impact upon the image of business, for it was held partly responsible for the collapse.

However, a prime contributing factor to the unpopularity of business is general ignorance on the part of the public of the role of business in a capitalist market economy. Sylvia Porter is correct in saying that economic illiteracy of the public is a fundamental threat to the survival of the free enterprise system in America.[2] For example, in a 1974 poll conducted by Opinion Research Corporation, the typical response was that corporate profits amount to 28 cents out of every dollar.[3] The actual average, at least for 1974, was 5.2 cents. Other polls tend to show that most Americans have only the vaguest idea of what profits really are or what they are supposed to accomplish in a free enterprise market economy. The basic cause of this economic illiteracy can be attributed to the educational system of the United States. In the high schools, few social studies teachers have had training in economics. In the colleges, there has been a tendency to distort the facts about free enterprise and business. But this in itself does not exonerate business, for it has done a rather poor job of selling itself to the public.

Forces supporting the private sector are today far more vulnerable politically than those pressing to diminish its role. The increasing power of politically active nonbusiness groups addressing environmental issues, product regulation, minority demands, feminist proposals, political reform, health programs, and so on hardly supports the claim that corporations dominate American life. The leading proponent of business deconcentration, the late Senator Phillip Hart, came from General Motors' home state. It is politically convenient to have a group to blame for society's ills and to divert attention from the weakness of one's own programs. As Huey Long once said, "Corporations are the finest enemies in the world." [4] Business is a magnet for attracting public discontent and becomes a mark for politicians who have no idea of what business is supposed to do or what profits mean to investment.

This is abundantly clear in the case of the oil industry, which earned the acrimony of most of the American public when abnormally high profits were reported for the third quarter of 1979. More than any single industry in the United States, the oil industry has come to occupy the attention and concern of public policy during the 1970s. There is an idea prevalent among consumer groups and at least a part of Congress that new antitrust laws are needed to regulate the oil industry.[5] Through mergers, domestic oil companies have extended their activities into other sources of energy—coal, uranium, and natural gas. Companies such as Mobil Oil, which acquired Montgomery Ward, have expanded into areas outside the field of energy. In the international area, the U.S. multinational oil companies stand accused of having achieved a monopoly over the world supply of oil, along with oil companies of other countries, and of having conspired to fix prices and restrict the supply of oil in world markets over an extended period of time.[6]

Recent polls illustrate the disenchantment of the public with the oil industry. A CBS-TV poll indicated that one-fourth of those persons polled favored outright nationalization of the oil industry and another one-third favored increased government regulation.[7] Another poll indicated that almost 70 percent of the public felt that the oil companies were lying when they said most of their high third-quarter profits were made from overseas sales.[8] Several polls have showed that a large majority of the public think that the energy shortage has been contrived by the oil companies in order to make money. The gasoline shortages of 1979 and the attendant long lines of automobiles at the pumps were blamed by the public on the oil companies, which were accused of withholding supplies in order to drive up the price of gasoline. The oil industry, then, stands indicted by the American public on many counts—some of them true and some of them false. It is now the lightning rod that attracts public discontent, and the quantum of public sympathy can be measured with a thimble.

Marshal Foch is reputed to have said during the Second Battle of the Marne, "My center is giving way, my right is pushed back, situation excellent, I am attacking." [9] Some modern football coaches say the same thing in a much more prosaic way: "The best defense is a good offense." Mobil Oil apparently decided to adhere to both dicta rather belatedly when it came out with the advertisement in *Time, Newsweek,* and other publications that said, "How CBS on October 24, 1979, Prefabricated the News." [10] October 24, 1979 was not exactly a redletter day for the oil industry, for Walter Cronkite started out the "CBS Evening News" as follows (copyright © 1979 CBS Inc. All rights reserved. Originally broadcast on "CBS Evening News" on October 24, 1979, over the CBS Television Network):

> WALTER CRONKITE: Good evening. Five more oil companies today reported huge profit increases for the third quarter, among them the giant Mobil, whose July-August-September profits were 131 percent higher than the same quarter last year. SOHIO reported a 191 percent gain, Sun was up 65 percent, CITGO up 64 percent and Marathon up 58 percent. Ray Brady reports.
>
> RAY BRADY: Mobil, like other international oil companies, says the big profits were not made here, but in foreign markets, which would mean that foreign consumers were the ones getting hit. Abroad, though, a top analyst of the world oil industry says that it is not necessarily so.

MARTIN BEUDELL (British Oil analyst): They are a great scape-goat in the U.S., the oil industry, the energy industry. So, you are inclined to do that, to deemphasize your home prof-its and stress what you make overseas.

RAY BRADY: American critics charge that it is simply a matter of bookkeeping, to earn a foreign profit from an American consumer.

EDWIN ROTHSCHILD (Energy Action Educational Foundation): Every time he buys a gallon of gasoline for a dollar a gallon, some of that profit is made in the United States, but the rest of the profits these companies earn is spread among their foreign subsidiaries.

RAY BRADY: Roughly 40 percent of our oil comes from abroad, about one-fifth of it already refined. The oil companies say there are limits on what they can charge, but critics say for $18 they can buy a barrel of oil in Saudi Arabia, then it might make the long trip to a refinery in the Caribbean, where they can sell it to their own subsidiary or another company for $25. After costs, the difference of $7 is profit —a foreign profit earned abroad. Once the oil is refined, it could go to the U.S., the critics go on, sold to a marketing firm for a price of, say, $35. After costs, the difference of $10 is more foreign profit. The oil companies argue that many of their profits go to their stockholders as dividends. The government would like to put a windfall profits tax on some of these profits earned in this country, but oil company critics say that would simply result in the oil companies com-ing up with more foreign profits.

After the reporting of this news, the oil companies were in the position of the White Star Line when it learned that the *Titanic* had sunk. The news could hardly have been expected to warm the hearts of American consumers toward the oil in-dustry. Moreover, it would have been stupid of the industry to assume otherwise. Anyway, Mobil stated in its two-page adver-tisement: "We should have seen this curveball coming, but we didn't." That is obvious, for Mobil struck out. The ad goes on to castigate CBS for allegedly prefabricating its report and at-tempts to set the record straight as far as Mobil's earnings were concerned. But the horse was already out of the barn. First, it is rather pointless to attack CBS, for it has more power. There was once a time when politicians could attack "lying news-papers" and get away with it. Those days are long since gone. When the power of the media is compared with that of the corporation, it cannot be seriously argued that the conscious influence on American life exerted by all the manufacturing corporations in the country is even remotely close to that exercised by a single television network.[11]

It can also be argued that the role of the corporation in consciously influencing American society is probably less important than that of the universities. The most, and usually the only, sustained and systematic exposure of many persons to underlying issues of public policies is in the universities, and academic opinion on public issues is usually slanted in one direction. In virtually every academic area, with the exceptions of engineering and business, professional opinion is openly antagonistic to the private sector and is pressing relentlessly for more and more government control. The long-standing tilt in American higher education has inevitably affected public opinion and is one of the basic causes of the enormous growth in government over the last forty to fifty years. The political outlook of university faculties has shaped what Irving Kristol calls the "new class" of journalists, academics, polemicists, public interest advocates, and so on.[12] This group, which has steadily grown in influence during this century, finds power in its ability to influence government—and influence government it does. In economics, an academic area that might be somewhat supportive of capitalism, supporters of private enterprise and a free market economy belong to the so-called Chicago school of economics, patterned after the apostle of free enterprise, Milton Friedman. But the Chicago school has little clout in most economics departments.

Mobil's battle for hearts and minds was lost before it was begun. It is doubtful that readers of *Time* and *Newsweek* are going to be influenced by the advertisement, even if they read it. What Mobil and other oil companies should have done a long time ago is attempt to educate the American public on the economics of the oil industry. Contact with universities should not be limited to recruiting graduates in engineering and geology. More effort should have been made to cultivate members

of the "new class," for their influence in government and politics is far disproportionate to their numbers. This effort, however, should not be limited to the oil industry. All corporations
have to do a better job of explaining the role of profit in a
capitalist economy. In private enterprise, profit is necessary for
survival: Anyone who produces things that do not, directly or
indirectly, yield a profit will sooner or later go bankrupt, lose
his ownership of the means of production, and so cease to
become an independent producer. There can be no other way,
for profit is the test of whether or not any given item should or
should not be produced.

Fortunately for business, a revisionist group of economists is
on the rise in academic and professional circles.[13] These economists, who are eclectic and unorthodox by past economic standards, argue that government is the cause of many of the
economic ills of contemporary society. They assert that government has motivated Americans to spend too much and save too
little. They charge that federal tax, budget, and monetary
policies have promoted immediate consumption instead of
investment for the future, and they argue for reduction
in government spending, particularly for unproductive social
programs. Personal initiative should be encouraged, and the
role of government in the economy should be reduced. Long-
term incentives should be given to encourage saving and investment by individuals and corporations, and, above all, supply and production should be stimulated and increased instead
of demand and consumption. Boosting supply may well be the
only long-run antidote to the problem of a decade of inflation,
the worst in American history.

Then there is the "new politics" or "new populism" of today,
which may or may not be a passing fancy.[14] This politics developed at the state level of government and is based on the reali-
ties of today—that times are tough, taxpayers are rebellious,
and problems are quite possibly insoluble by government intervention. The premise of the "new politics" is that humans and
all their works, including government, are limited, and that the
proper object of power is only to reduce the sum of human
misery, not to try to program it away altogether with money,
data readouts, and systems analysis. The idea that solutions can

be bought for any problem has encouraged overpromising by government and inflated the expectations of the governed. The latter can be dangerous, for a psychology of rising expectations can lead to social discontent if the expectations are not gratified.

The Business Advocacy Approach

What business needs is a more effective advocacy approach to improve its relations with government and the public. Pamphlets to stockholders and advertisements in newspapers extolling the virtues of the free enterprise system will hardly make a dent in the public distrust of business. Business sniping at government, as reflected in a number of advertisements that have appeared in major magazines and newspapers, has little impact. For example, in *Industry Week,* a business firm ran a full-page ad listing what it considered to be wasteful expenditures for such projects as "A Study of Polish Bisexual Frogs" and "A Study of Brothels in Lima, Peru." [15] There is, of course, a parallel between this ad and the Golden Fleece Award of Senator William Proxmire of Wisconsin.[16] Nevertheless, the approach is rather quixotic, for although it may gain attention, it causes little or no change in the way government works. What is needed is a systematic advocacy approach to problems that affect the basic functions of business—production, research, and marketing.

The relationship of business and government is changing. A few trend-setting business firms are beginning to assume an advocacy role with respect to government and society. An Atlantic-Richfield (Arco) ad that appeared in *Time* stated, "I'm giving my Congressman hell. I'm telling him to quit the fancy maneuvering and the politicking and to get about the business of some kind of national energy policy." [17] The advocacy approach makes sense, for American business cannot be expected to be successful in waging a two-front war, struggling against increased government encroachment at home while competing against government-supported enterprises abroad. When the business point of view is presented well, it often has proved to be successful. During the last two years, business was able to lobby effectively against bills that would have allowed common-situs picketing, established a consumer protection agency, and expanded union power through labor law reform.[18] The momentum, at least for the present, is on the side of the business advocates. Energy and expense are effectively directed at issues that affect business profitability.

The business advocacy approach can be divided into five major areas: internal, external, general public information, political involvement, and public policy research. It is desirable to provide some elaboration on each category, for individual companies have limited resources and must focus on activities that will best meet their own needs and responsibilities. In recent years, many business firms have attempted to reach into all five areas, sometimes with less than impressive results.

The Internal Approach

The internal approach encompasses customer education, employee education and training, and stockholder education. Gulf Oil Corporation provides a "Gulf Consumer News Digest," which it sends to its customers. This type of direct communication with customers is also fairly common within the food industry. Supermarket chains such as Giant Foods and Safeway have made efforts to produce consumer education materials that will assist customers. Most often these activities focus on the quality of a product or identify how a person might make his views known to the business involved. Sometimes consumer education may be indirectly related to a product. An example is Shell Oil's popular ad series, "Come to Shell for Answers," which provides information ranging from home security to car repairs but does not tout the product itself.

Employee education and training attempt to provide a framework for employee participation in political activities. Dow Chemical and Whirlpool have produced government affairs programs for their employees. The Dow Chemical program, "It's Your Government, Too," [19] and Whirlpool's "Government Workshop" present video and written material to be used in small discussion groups among employees. Emphasis is placed on legislation and other government activities that have a direct impact on business activities. Although slanted to present the business point of view, these programs are no more biased than those presented by labor unions and other special interest groups.

Stockholder education is a third example of the internal approach. Many companies communicate with their stockholders concerning the activities of government. This communication can appear in the annual stockholders' report; more typically it appears in the form of a letter or memorandum from the president of the company. In the General Motors annual report for 1976, reference is made to an investigation of the American automobile industry that is to be made by the Federal Trade Commission.[20] Concern over this investigation is reflected in a section of the report called "Competition in the Automobile Industry," in which General Motors argues that the automobile industry is and always has been competitive. General Motors touts the virtues of the American economic system—freedom of enterprise, freedom of consumer choice, and competition. The American consumer has many choices: He can buy from General Motors, from its competitors, or not buy at all. The message to General Motors stockholders is clear: The Federal Trade Commission is in error if it thinks the automobile industry is not competitive.

The External Approach

The external approach includes community development, business and government activities, and international relations. In the area of community development, Honeywell has a program called "Community Action," in which community service activities are stressed. IBM has three programs dealing directly with community services, and Xerox has a community involvement program. A merit of community development activities is that they improve the public's image of business. Business appears to be interested in other things over and above making a profit, and projects itself as being a part of the community.

Business and government relations involve all levels of government—federal, state, and local. Probably the most impor-

tant business activity is lobbying. Many corporations have
Washington offices and belong to trade associations and national organizations that represent their interests before Congress and at state and local levels of government. Business
lobbyists show materials that present a business or organizational view about a particular legislative issue or a broad policy
area. For example, the Institute of Scrap Iron and Steel presented to congressional staff members a film and packet of
materials dealing with scrap processing, with particular emphasis placed on conservation. Public officials and their staffs often
find this type of activity to be useful in their legislative or executive activities.

Most large corporations are multinational, meaning that they
carry on their activities on an international scale, as though
there were no international barriers. There is a great deal of
ambivalence concerning the impact of multinational corporations. To some persons, they represent a worldwide unifying
force that will ultimately replace the outmoded interests of existing nation-states; to others, they represent a sinister force
that could lead to world economic and political dominance by
a few firms. American business firms with operations abroad
are stressing the benefits that accrue to the host and American
economies. Occidental Petroleum likes to point out that it is
solving the U.S. energy shortage by drilling for petroleum in
other countries. U.S. laws that supposedly place American
multinational firms at a competitive disadvantage in world markets are subject to challenge by these firms.

General Public Information

The dissemination of public information is viewed as highly
desirable by many business firms. For example, U.S. Steel has
produced a series of essays called "What Makes America
Work?" These essays are written by major national figures from
labor, management, and the academic community who are invited to respond to various subjects. The series appears in popular magazines, and its advertisements are in color and
generally spread across two pages. The Koss Corporation produces a pamphlet entitled "Free Enterprise: Getting Back to

Basics." Mobil Oil has produced newspaper ads focusing on the natural gas shortage that state "It's up to Congress Now." There is merit to the public policy approach, for it is necessary for business to present its views to the general public. John L. Lewis, the guiding light of the United Mine Workers Union for many years, said, "He who doesn't toot his own horn, doesn't get it tooted." Labor has done an excellent job over the years of tooting its horn. Business needs to do the same, but perhaps less blatantly. An educational approach is desirable strategy.

Political Involvement

The attitude of business toward political affairs has generally been Olympian for most of this century. Politics was considered rather crass, and businessmen just didn't want to be involved. However, the role of organized labor in politics is well recognized. An issue of the *United Steel Workers Journal* makes note of the role of the union in supporting consumer bills introduced in the Pennsylvania legislature.[21] Organized labor has backed up its advocacy of special legislation with substantial political contributions, including financial support of candidates and the provision of thousands of volunteers. The United Paperworkers International Union sponsors a political education program that is supported by a "voluntary" contribution from each member. During the presidential campaign of 1976, organized labor spent an estimated $11 million to help the Carter-Mondale ticket. This amount can be compared to the $21.8 million in federal funds that the Democratic ticket could legally spend. In addition, organized labor engaged in a massive voter registration campaign and saw to it that on election day registered voters got to the polling places. In a close election, labor support was decisive for Carter-Mondale.

Business firms are beginning to encourage their employees, stockholders, and customers to become more involved in politics. The National Association of Manufacturers has suggested that its members encourage their employees and stockholders to register and vote, and allow political candidates to tour company offices or plants.[22] Members are encouraged to state their position on issues affecting their well-being, and to sponsor programs and seminars explaining how to be effective in politics. Business firms may also grant voluntary leaves of absence to employees who wish to work in political campaigns. One basic rationale of business participation in politics is that it is necessary for it to create a political constituency of its own. A meaningful political power base requires both votes and money. In our affluent society, money is not lacking for any interest with a good-sized bloc of votes. It would be wrong to discourage businessmen from contributing to political candidates, for the exercise of political power requires the ability to provide inputs.

William G. Whyte, a vice-president of U.S. Steel, has outlined a four-point public affairs advocacy program. He recommends that top management decide to get involved, assign someone at each company plant to be responsible for public affairs, increase participation in local, state, and national political affairs, and participate financially to the extent the law allows.[23] Fred B. Zoll, vice-president of Libby-Owens-Ford, states that the American businessman is an endangered species. This none-too-sanguine remark is based on the fact that the business community has been living in what amounts to a political power vacuum. The utilitarian business ethic has only rarely been able to stir emotions and to rally a politically useful voting bloc to its cause. But it is not impossible for business to enlist the support of investors, employees, and customers if the right approaches are used. There had been an absence of political competence within the business organizations, an inability to generate voting support for a political position affecting their interest.

Political involvement on the part of business can be party-oriented or issue-oriented. With party distinctions often blurred, particularly in the South, many business firms have found it desirable to concentrate on issues affecting their interests. In one of its publications, Boise Cascade urged its employees and stockholders to judge political candidates on stands taken on issues affecting the company.[24] The chairman of the board of Alcoa, in a letter to company stockholders, asks that they write or telephone their senators and representatives concerning issues related to the interest of the company.[25] Opposition is urged to legislation that would alter the present rules with respect to the taxation of foreign income, and support is urged for the elimination of double taxation of dividends. The chairman of Union Carbide testified before the Senate Finance Committee in support of the foreign tax credit, stating that its repeal would seriously affect the ability of U.S. corporations to compete with foreign companies.[26] Exxon has also taken the initiative in its *Happy Motoring News,* in which it extolls the efficiency of private enterprise in handling solutions to the energy problem.[27]

Public Policy Research

A number of business firms have begun to support public policy research organizations such as the American Enterprise Institute and the Brookings Institution. The American Enterprise Institute has produced a series of Public Policy Forums which deal with a variety of domestic and foreign issues.[28] These forums are taped and are made available to educational television, radio stations, libraries, and any interested group. In addition, scholars from leading academic institutions provide monographs and position papers on a variety of subjects. There is a special study series dealing with government regulation of public utilities.[29] One study analyzes the effectiveness of the Federal Trade Commission with respect to regulation of business. The Brookings Institution also provides quality public policy research. It, too, has made extensive studies of the impact of government regulation upon business.[30] The public policy research of the American Enterprise Institute and Brookings can provide decision makers with information based on an analysis of policy alternatives in a decision environment characterized by multiple interests, conflicting objectives, and a strong interaction between means and ends.

The Committee for Economic Development, the Rand Corporation, and the Conference Board also provide public policy research. The Committee for Economic Development is an association of business firms that produces position papers on a variety of issues, including tax policy, economic growth, and monetary policy. The Rand Corporation has assisted the City of New York with some of its urban administration problems.

At a time when construction targets were not being met and the demand for additional housing was rising rapidly, it was asked to furnish a cheaper and faster way to provide public housing. The Conference Board not only sponsors public policy research, but also provides businessmen with an opportunity to participate directly in making public policy decisions. In 1975, a congressional assistantship program was established to provide highly qualified executives, nominated and supported by the board, to serve on one-year assignments as staff assistants on congressional committees.[31] Participants in 1977 included executives from Bell Telephone, General Foods, Corning Glass, Prudential, and General Motors. In creating this program, the Conference Board recognized the increasing need for interaction between the private sector and government.

Clemenceau once said that war is too important to be left to the generals. By the same token, public policy research is too important to be left to the federal government, the prime sponsor and performer of policy research. Business firms can realize several benefits from sponsoring public policy research. First, research can focus attention on subjects of special interest to business where government has less interest. Second, both means and ends are subject to careful analysis, and third, policy research can promote positive changes. The private sector has a large stake in public policies, and gaps in knowledge are a continuing deterrent to good public policy. Although the private sector has the capacity and resources to support public policy research, it has defaulted, leaving sponsorship and utilization to the federal government, with some assistance from private institutions such as those mentioned above. Many areas of research, however, do not fall within the charter of any one federal agency or private institution.

There are several important areas of public policy research that are of current interest to business. One such area involves the apparent decline in U.S. productivity relative to other nations. Real growth in gross national product has been lower in the United States than it has been in Japan and West Germany in recent years. Labor productivity in the United States increased by 2.8 percent in 1978 compared to a productivity increase of 8.3 percent for Japan.[32] Why is the rate of increase in U.S. productivity dropping? Is it because of a decline in the work ethic or because of the current emphasis on egalitarianism and equality of representation? Perhaps it is caused by excessive government regulations. Import barriers support such ailing industries as steel and textiles, and inefficient firms are sometimes kept alive by federal financial assistance. Low productivity can also be caused by inadequate investment on the part of business. No one seems to know what has caused the decline in productivity, but there is an awareness that productivity is indeed a problem.

Research could also be concentrated on tax policy and the problem of low capital investment, which are related to the productivity problem. The congressional bipartisan Joint Economic Committee issued a warning in its 1979 midyear report: Unless major improvements are made in expanding the supply side of the economy, by boosting savings and investment in order to lift productivity, the nation will face a drastically declining standard of living in the 1980s.[33] Technological progress is the prime determinant of the rate of growth in productivity, but it is necessary to know the most efficient ways of making new technology available, and to create new incentives for its adoption in industry. Business-sponsored research can also provide a better knowledge base for economic policy pertaining to such areas as energy, urban development, and transportation.[34] Nearly all social issues can benefit from increased information about policy choices and their consequences.

Business Should Get Involved

The utilitarian business ethic has only rarely been able to stir emotions and to rally a politically useful voting bloc to its cause. Government, to the contrary, can engage in political predation against, say, the oil industry, with no risk of any such adverse reaction as can result from a like attack upon the interests of firearm users. Few politicians want to take on the National Rifle Association, even though its membership is probably less than the number of employees and stockholders of any one of the major oil companies. Although they have not been in the news lately, even Tom Hayden and Jane Fonda have been known to exert more influence upon public opinion than the president of General Motors. Their message to the public is simple: Everything that is wrong with the world, from nuclear fallout to the Pope's refusal to ordain women into the priesthood, is the fault of greedy American businessmen seeking profits. Put us in charge, and you will achieve nirvana. They have found an audience, and business has not, a situation that now seems to be reversing itself.

Calvin Coolidge once said, "The business of America is business."[35] His sentiment was reflective of American values during a bygone period when Horatio Alger stories epitomized the glories of the Protestant work ethic. However, the halcyon years of business ended long ago, and since World War II, great changes in the American social order have altered the domestic balance of power between business and other groups. A "new class," concentrated in the universities, and in particular in the communications industry, has emerged and has attempted to impose what can be called a "new morality" upon American society. This new elite is statist in orientation and maintains an adversarial posture against the central concepts of our political, cultural, and economic system. Its attitude toward business can perhaps be summarized in this way: "What's bad for business is good for the country and vice versa." [36] The "new class" has chosen the power of government, particularly that of the federal government, as the preferred instrument of change, and in the process it has created a reservoir of political power in various groups who depend upon government spending—government workers, social workers, educational institutions, and workers in those industries whose economic base depends upon large government spending.

The exercise of political leverage on the part of business requires communication between business and the public and between business and government on significant economic and social issues. Although business has improved its communications with both groups, much remains to be done. It is necessary for business, not just big business, to learn to deal more effectively with all levels of government, in particular the federal government. All too often, government expertise on economic matters is derived from academia, consulting firms, and legislative staffs rather than business, which is more likely to be directly involved in the economy. Academicians usually have an axe to grind, consulting firms have gotten rich off government contracts, and legislative staffs are not necessarily qualified to provide expert judgment on issues of importance to business.

There appears to be a growing adverse reaction to excess government regulation. Congress is mounting a broad attack on a system the legislators themselves created. For example, the Senate Commerce Committee voted overwhelmingly to keep the Federal Trade Commission (FTC) out of such areas as children's television advertising, used car lots, the insurance industry, and consumer product standards. Through amendments to the FTC's authorization bill, the committee also sharply curtailed the ability of the FTC to issue subpoenas and fund public participation in agency proceedings. The shifting attitude toward government regulation can be attributed to a number of factors, not the least of which is the high cost of excessive government regulation, most of which is borne by consumers. Increased lobbying efforts on the part of business are certainly a factor, although it is to be doubted that business has as much power as consumer and environmentalist groups think it has. Another factor is that many regulatory agencies have exceeded the authority given to them by Congress. As mentioned previously, business has no alternative but to comply with regulations and social goals, since most regulatory agencies have sufficient enforcement tools.

In summary, it is apparent that business has to develop new political strategies involving more effective communication. There is a certain amount of ideological warfare involved, and business, at least in the past, has not been prepared to enter the lists in the war of ideas. As was mentioned previously, there is the need to enlist or at least encourage support from universities and independent intellectual groups such as the American Enterprise Institute and the Brookings Institution. Business also has to take a greater initiative in challenging opposing accusations and ideologies developed by other groups. It is often difficult for business to articulate its positions effectively in a way designed to meet hostile attack. Then it is also necessary to organize more effectively in dealing with government. If nothing else, business should at least be aware of long-range issues of government that will impact upon business activity. It can be done by creating a small staff of issue watchers. More important, however, is a concrete organization for managing government relations. This is the subject of the next chapter.

5

Managing the Government Relations Function

> The main problems of business these days are external to the company and are determined in the arena of public policy. Therefore business managers are obliged to become students of public affairs. They must know how to hold their own in public debate and know their way around in Washington. When business managers bring their experience to bear in the formation of policy and law, they speak for millions of affected people and deserve a hearing.[1]

The above statement, made by Reginald Jones, president of General Electric, is quite true. For an extended period of time, the views of business have not carried much weight in the public policy process. Costly programs to protect the environment, provide more jobs for women and minorities, enforce safety standards for consumer products, and create safer working conditions have been passed over the objections of business—and largely without regard to their impact on the economy.[2]

In the development of public policy, the advantage has been held, at least until now, by well-organized groups such as organized labor, Common Cause, environmentalists, and Ralph Nader's consumerists. An accumulation of antibusiness bias and ingrained social attitudes has continued to spell trouble for business. Therefore, it is desirable for business to discontinue its adversary relationship with government and think in terms of an advocacy role. This involves an active participation in congressional and other political activities. The public concern with such issues as ecology, equal employment opportunity, and consumer protection may, in retrospect, be the result of social change that has been occurring in the United States during the last decade. However, few companies devoted time and resources during this time to diagnose or prepare for a more complicated political and social environment. New forces in many instances have constrained existing strategies; sometimes they have called for revisions, and often they have entailed higher costs.

Minimizing Adverse Regulation

In today's world the best management of traditional business functions will not guarantee profit; hence, there is a need to focus on the government relations function as a major factor affecting corporate profitability. The relevant strategy is to try to minimize the adverse effects of administrative and bureaucratic regulation. The decision points are visible, and it is clear whose ox will be gored if business remains aloof from the political decision-making process as it has in the past. The places to begin are where the laws affecting business are made, namely, in Congress and in the state legislatures. The time for action is propitious. There is the feeling on the part of Congress that many administrative agencies have usurped its authority to make laws. In fact, Congress recently emasculated the regulative authority of the Federal Trade Commission, feeling that it had clearly overstepped its boundaries. Congressional proposals to check the spread of regulation include the one-house veto, formal presidential intervention in agency rule-making procedures, and more active judicial review. In all cases, the aim of Congress is to find ways to second-guess the broad, detailed public policy formulation and the development of alternative solutions to social and economic problems.

In order to become more involved in the making of a public policy, a business firm must acknowledge and improve its management of the functional relationship between government and business.[3] Systematic attention to managing this functional relationship can result in improved corporate profitability by eliminating duplication of government relations efforts. Constant monitoring of government action can also result in more responsible governance and assist in the continuation and improvement of the American form of government. There must be a willingness on the part of business to get out and argue effectively for what it believes. If it does not, who will? The cartoon character Pogo once said, "We have met the enemy, and they is us." This applies to business so appropriately, for business is often its own worst enemy when it comes to public relations. Conventional public relations and pejorative pronouncements usually have very little impact upon Congress, much less change its and the public's perception of the purpose of business in American life.

Political factors have become vastly more important to business in recent years, as the federal government has created a number of new regulatory agencies that have let loose upon business an unprecedented number of rules and regulations. Like the Hydra of Greek mythology, which could grow two heads for each one that was lopped off by Hercules, the new regulatory agencies, such as the Occupational Safety and Health Administration, and their older cousins, like the Federal Trade Commission, have come up with two rules for every rule eliminated. Corporate chief executives have found themselves devoting more and more of their time to issues raised by government agencies. Rare nowadays are the managers who can ignore the political consequences of their decisions or the impact of public policy on future decisions. Some of the elements that influence the strategic policymaking equation have been with business for years, such as tariffs and other trade restrictions or antitrust regulation. Most, however, surfaced in the seventies, either through private action in the courts or at stockholders' meetings, or through rules by which regulators try to control business.

Questions That Need to Be Answered

It is incumbent upon business to adopt new and more productive techniques for dealing with government—techniques that include negotiation and providing information to government decision makers. The ability to communicate effectively is a vital ingredient in the successful implementation of any management strategy involving government. Thus, it is necessary for business to develop a functional relationship with government that can involve prescribed rules of management. A series of key management questions can direct attention to the crucial components of managing the government relations function. These questions, once answered, can provide insight concerning the management of this function. The questions and their answers are presented below.

Who Should Manage Government Relations?

The answer to this question is that it depends upon the size of the firm. Small firms may rely upon a chief executive officer, a trade association, or perhaps an attorney or accountant retained as a consultant to help make management decisions. Usually a trade association will suffice. For large firms, a vice-president or manager for public relations should be designated to handle the day-to-day implementation of a government relations plan. This person should report to and work directly with the chief executive officer of the company. It is to be expected that he or she be adept at public relations, for a certain amount of savoir faire and charisma is necessary in dealing with the legislators who make laws and the bureaucrats who enforce them. A public relations problem confronting business is its facelessness. It is much easier to accept a business point of view if there is a human being attached to it. It is also to be expected that the person designated to manage government relations have considerable expertise concerning not only existing legislation affecting business, but pending legislation as well.

However, a government relations manager cannot act alone, for there is the need, at various points, to obtain support from members of the corporate community. He or she must have direct access to the chief executive officer in order to initiate communication with consumers, employees, and stockholders. Consumers and stockholders are company constituents, and as government constituents, they elect representatives to serve them at the local, state, and federal levels of government. Employees deal with business and government as private citizens. Moreover, as insiders, they are concerned with sales, marketing, personnel administration, manufacturing, product design and development, engineering, and numerous other business functions. It is necessary for the government relations manager to identify issues that are of concern to company constituents. For example, stockholders are mainly concerned about earning an adequate rate of return on their investment, and any government action that impinges upon this return is bound to attract their interest.

The issues that employees, stockholders, and consumers face in their insider and outsider roles are multifarious. These include marketing practices, product line standards, employee education and training, corporate philanthropy, environmental control, employee benefits, affirmative action, and safety and health standards. From a government relations perspective, the major issues are product liability, consumer protection, equal employment opportunity, taxes, environmental protection, and occupational safety. The list goes on and on, with new issues appearing almost on a monthly basis. All of these issues require company time, for they affect profit. The manager of government relations should coordinate the responses to these issues. He or she can make an inventory of government relations issues, make systematic decisions about attempting to influence the drafting of government legislation or questioning regulations inimical to business, and make systematic decisions about dollars to be spent, man-hours to be allocated, and activities to be emphasized.

Figure 5.1 presents how one company, General Foods, handles public and government relations. Public affairs, public relations, and government relations are combined under a vice-president for public relations/public affairs, who reports to the vice-chairman of the company. Stockholder and instutional relations are the responsibility of the financial department of General Foods. Consumer relations and product publicity in women's interest media are under the jurisdiction of the vice-president for consumer affairs, while public relations handles product publicity in trade and general media. There is a close working relationship, however, between public relations and the people who handle both consumer affairs and investor relations. The vice-president of public relations/public affairs sits on committees with the functional heads of the other areas to formulate policy and to develop joint programs.

Other companies may choose to handle government relations differently. At a major oil company, the vice-president of public affairs has direct responsibility for planning and coordinating all corporate communications. Government is a part of public affairs, reflecting the fact that oil companies have to place special emphasis on external relations growing out of the increasing government and public interest in the oil industry. The company has a vice-president, Washington office, who is directly under the vice-president of public affairs. There is also a manager of government and industry affairs, who is responsible to the vice-president of public affairs. The manager is responsible for coordinating federal, state, and local government relations. The oil company uses an organizational approach to external affairs used by a number of companies in that there is a designated executive who is responsible for all external relations of the company-government relations (federal, state, and local), consumer relations, and stockholder and institutional investor relations. This executive is responsible to the chief executive officer of the company. An advantage of coordinating all external activities under one executive is that consistency is critical to effective external relations: The company must speak with one voice.

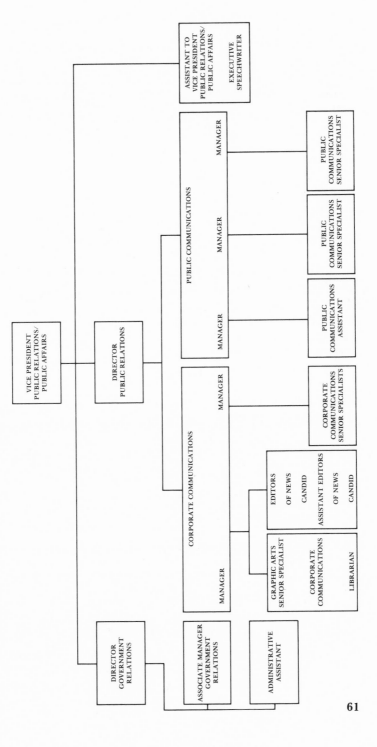

FIGURE 5.1 **Combining Public Relations, Public Affairs, and Government Relations—General Foods Corporation.** *From Phyllis S. McGrath, Managing Corporate External Relations: Changing Perspectives and Responses, New York: The Conference Board, 1976, p. 31. Used with permission.*

How Can Business Best Manage Government Relations?

After assigning corporate responsibility for managing government relations, various factors have to be kept in mind. An inventory should be made of various issues and categories of government activities that have an impact upon corporate profits. By overlaying these components, a business-government interface map can be developed. This map leads to an agenda-setting stage in which a company determines its goals and sets priorities for action. For example, it may determine that specific pending federal legislation is a problem area that requires immediate attention. To assist in legislative lobbying, if it does not have a Washington office, the company may decide to establish one.[4] Corporate personnel and stockholders can be informed of the pending legislation and asked to call or write their congressmen. Trade groups can be encouraged to organize a campaign to confront the problem. In any case, it is important for a company to have a goal and a strategy. No general can afford to go into battle without a battle plan; no company can afford to neglect a plan to deal with government policies that vitally affect its operations. To do so is to court disaster. The development of a business-government interface map provides for a plan of action.

When Do You Manage the Government Relations Function?

The answer to this question is timely communication. The government relations manager has to be aware of the levels and processes of government, as well as the various points of access.[5] By overlaying corporate problems on this matrix while reviewing company goals and priorities, the government relations manager is in a position to administer a planned government relations strategy. In practice, the manager may have contact with business groups such as the Chamber of Commerce and the National Association of Manufacturers, and also with research and information support organizations. In addition, he or she will be in contact with persons at various levels of government. It is desirable for the manager to have the authority to initiate immediate communication with the heads of operating departments within his or her company, including such areas as product development, sales, marketing, personnel, manufacturing, and engineering. Timely response by these departments is a key determinant of the government relations manager's effectiveness.

It is not uncommon for senior corporate executives, government relations personnel, and trade association members to take an active role in attempting to influence legislative policymaking. Individuals representing corporations and other organizations provide most of the information and analysis, and thus influence the creation of public policy. Government decision makers are dependent on these individuals for information that would never be discovered through government research procedures. But most of these efforts are poorly timed, lack specific corporate reference, or are not part of an organized plan.

Timely relay of information is one of the cardinal rules for successful influence in both legislative and other executive and regulatory lobbying. For instance, an executive of Anaconda Company recently received a letter from his senator:

> Dear Mr. Cyr:
>
> I appreciate your position asking me to sustain the President's veto of S. 391, the Mineral Leasing Act, and understand your concern. However, as you know, I voted to override the veto.
>
> When the bill passed the Senate over a year ago, I supported it, not having heard one expression of opposition to it. When a drastically revised version passed the House, I still had not received a word against it, and I believe it was because of this silence that the bill did not go to a House-Senate conference. Very few, if any, of us had been advised of its adverse effects as seen by some. I heard opposing views only after the President had vetoed the legislation and, frankly, by then it was too late.
>
> I rely heavily on information relayed to me from my constituents, private industry, and other groups, but I cannot act on it if I am not advised in a timely fashion.[6]

The most effective government relations manager also has a direct communication link with the chief executive officer. With the chief executive officer's approval, he or she can initiate timely communication with the corporation's stockholders, employees, and consumers.

Effective communication is a vital ingredient in the successful implementation of any management strategy. If the government relations function is to be systematically controlled and assist company profitability, the government relations communication network must be developed to its full potential. Using this network, the government relations manager must, in a timely manner, organize, plan, define goals and purposes, select means, give direction, control, motivate, energize, reward, measure, and report on the various components of government relations.

What Is to Be Done?

This is the key to improving company profitability. A well-managed, coordinated strategy will increase the chances that legislation and other government action will not, either in the short term or the long term, reduce company profitability. Frankly, one company's effort will rarely make much of a difference at the federal level; typically, a few trend-setting companies, with the support of their trade associations, encourage responsible government action. But at the state and local government levels, a single company can make a difference. For example, a company can often obtain tax concessions from a state or local government for establishing new plants or facilities within a specific jurisdiction.

A systematic approach to the basic problems that confront the organization should be developed. A "personalized" company strategy for managing government relations is based on the awareness of problems, formulation of issue categories to be treated, assignment of responsibility, and resource allocation.

The stages of corporate awareness of government-related problems seem to be:

Stage 1: What is the government doing to us?
Stage 2: What might the government do to us?
Stage 3: Why don't we think this through?
Stage 4: We are going to take action.

The most common reaction to the discovery of a government requirement or intended action is the response "What are you [government] doing to me?" This reaction is often accompanied by disbelief, anger, and eventually a feeling of helplessness. No organization can entirely bypass this. But by asking the question "What might government do to us?" and planning and implementing a government relations strategy, a company can reduce the number of times it has to ask the former question.

After a company finds that the government wants it to do something, the normal tendency is to try to think through the problem. In thinking through the problem, many times the response will be "I guess we have to comply." It will be decided that some definite action needs to be taken. Action requires that goals and purposes be defined. Once the goals and purposes are defined, the circularity of the stages of awareness becomes obvious. Often the statement of goals and purposes will be followed by planning, which in turn will result in the rediscovery of "What might government do to us?"

A company, in reviewing the problems it faces, will develop issue categories that constitute the government-corporate interface.[7] Examples of these categories include marketing practices, product line liability, political campaign financial appeals, pensions, employee education and training, corporate philanthropy, environmental control, employee benefits, affirmative action, employee safety and health, taxation, and zoning. After breaking down the various components of these issues and determining which are most pressing, the allocation of corporate resources and assignment of corporate responsibility can begin.

Answering these questions will help corporations to manage the government relations function. Each answer provides insight, and together the answers form the foundation for efficient, effective corporate action. The tendency of government to compel business firms to shoulder the costs of carrying out a wide variety of social programs has burdened American business in international competition and has attenuated the private enterprise system. Today's society takes collective action to impose institutional constraints upon the production system. As our society gets richer and its goals become more complex, conflicts will become more difficult to resolve. It is utopian to think that we can have a cooperative relationship between business and government that is totally free from conflict, but it is possible to build a relationship that is better than the one that currently exists.

Finally, it is possible to think systematically about the government relations function. The time has come to plan and account for the government relations activity, as the manufacturing, marketing, and product development functions have been accounted for within the corporation. Government relations can be managed profitably as well as responsibly. Ignorance of the mechanics of government can have a deleterious effect upon corporate profitability. There is also an ignorance on the part of government officials about the competitive imperatives and the market discipline to which business firms are subject. The leaders of both institutions require a fuller education on the differences, as well as the similarities, of leadership roles in business and government. Government certainly can use better information from the private sector in order to formulate more effective economic and social policies, particularly in regard to the problems that lie ahead. The energy crisis is an example. As our society becomes more complex, its problems are going to be more difficult to resolve.

In subsequent chapters, the American system of government will be discussed in terms of a mechanism for making and administering business regulations. Emphasis will be placed on two institutions of government that have the greatest impact upon business—the U.S. Congress and the administrative agencies of the federal government. Congress makes the laws and has far-reaching authority to control most types of business activities, with the exception of those that are purely intrastate. There is, however, an overlap in many situations between what is considered interstate commerce and what is considered intrastate commerce.[8] Administrative agencies are so important that they have been called a "fourth branch of government," and the United States has been described as an "administrative state." Administrative agencies are defined as governmental bodies, other than courts and legislatures, that carry out the administrative tasks of government and affect the rights of private parties through adjudication and rule making. Every type of business enterprise in the United States falls within the jurisdiction or indirect influence of a number of administrative agencies.

Organized groups, including business, often seek to bring their influence directly upon members of Congress. Their goal is to shape government legislation along the lines of their interest. If they lose in Congress, they can appeal to the administrative agencies and then to the courts. If by chance they lose again, they frequently return to Congress in a final effort to modify the law or policy that limits their activities. These groups also have a vital concern in the work of state legislatures, for many laws affecting business or labor originate at the state level. State and local governments were the first to pass laws to protect the interests of consumers. Sanitary regulations, inspection of weights and measures, and the like were established state functions at the beginning of the nation's history. States were the first to pass antitrust and public utility regulation.[9] In fact, state antitrust laws have accelerated during the 1970s, in part because of a growing belief that the federal government cannot and should not bear full responsibility for the enforcement of antitrust. States and localities also have fair employment and environmental laws.

6

The Political
System

LIKE IT OR NOT (and most business firms don't), most decisions
affecting business emanate from Washington. It is all perfectly
legal. The Constitution of 1789 gave Congress the right to regulate commerce with foreign nations, among the several states,
and with the Indian tribes. Although the states are now more
than several, and the Indian tribes have gone the way of John
Wayne movies, the principle remains the same: Congress has
the power to regulate commerce. Its function is to make such
rules as it finds necessary and desirable to control the conduct
of business activity. The power to regulate, at least as it is applied to Congress, is the same as the power to govern. Courts
have broadly interpreted the power to regulate and have concluded that Congress may regulate activities having an effect
on interstate commerce in addition to regulating activities directly involving interstate commerce. Congress has no authority to regulate purely intrastate activities having no effect on
interstate commerce. However, even the most insignificant
local business probably has contact with or an effect on interstate commerce.

On the basis of experiences in the Depression, organized labor, farmers, and consumer groups have increasingly turned to government for assistance in improving their incomes and economic security. The satisfaction of these demands has made for a new concept of government. In the historical development of the United States, government policy was primarily an admixture of measures that provided equality of opportunity for the common man, such as public education, and generous favors for those who knew how to help themselves. But now government is disposed toward being the setter of our sights and the arbiter of our needs. Changes in fundamental values, symbols, ideals, and perceptions have greatly affected the climate in which business has to operate. Until recently, the climate of ideas and the business climate seemed to affect each other sympathetically. This is no longer the case. New special interest groups have developed that are openly hostile to the interests of business. Some of these groups view business as an obstacle to the sort of ideal society they wish to create. The best way to achieve their objectives is to put pressure on government by influencing public opinion. This is easily done through access to television and newspapers.

The United States possesses what can be called a "marble cake" government. With the exception of West Germany, the United States is unique in that it has a federal form of government that is divided into three parts—federal, state, and local. For the most part, the activities of these units complement each other, with each presumably performing the functions for which it is best suited. Examples of this arrangement are the federal government's control of currency and foreign relations and its maintenance of the armed forces. States have assumed part of the cost of education and highway maintenance, once exclusively local. Local governments provide fire and police protection and sanitary facilities. Occasionally, two government bodies cover the same function. All three levels of government have a direct impact upon business through the process of taxation and through the passage of laws that impose various forms of regulation. However, of the three levels, the federal government is clearly dominant in terms of its impact upon business, for it has more enumerated powers that bear directly upon the operation of the American economic system.[1]

The Constitution of the United States provides for a distribution of power among the legislative, executive, and judicial branches of government. This provision was made to prevent an undue concentration of power within the national government, and thus protect personal liberties and private property. An additional restriction on the exercise of political power was subsequently developed in the practice of judicial review. Soon after the federal courts began to function, they faced the question of whether or not certain acts of Congress were in harmony with the Constitution. In 1803, in the famous case of *Marbury* v. *Madison,* the Supreme Court held that a clause of the Judiciary Act of 1789 was contrary to the Constitution.[2] By this action the Court established a precedent for the enforcement of only those statutes passed by Congress that in its opinion are in accordance with the Constitution.

Legislative Branch

Mark Twain once made the statement that there is no distinctly American criminal class except Congress.[3] Will Rogers was a little more circumspect when he said that Congress had the best comedy act in Washington.[4] The American public apparently believes that both men have a point, for they have assigned to Congress a level of personal approval only slightly higher than that assigned to used car salesmen, and below that assigned to big business and organized labor. In fact, a recent Gallup poll gave Congress a public approval rating of 13 percent, an all-time low. In part, this low rating reflects public disenchantment with American institutions, which is a carry-over from the turbulent 1960s. Probably more important is the public perception of Congress as a body of self-serving politicians, voting themselves handsome pay raises while being at least partly responsible for the double-digit inflation that the United States is experiencing.

Nevertheless, there is no concerted effort on the part of the public to "throw the rascals out" and replace them with another set of politicians. In fact, the majority of congressmen are pretty much assured of a job for as long as they want it. Congress is the most important legislative body in the land. It passes the laws with which business and the general public have to contend. Since there are only 100 senators and 435 representatives for a country of 220 million persons, each member of Congress has considerable influence in the legislative process. Sources of ideas for legislation are unlimited, and proposed drafts of bills can originate from many diverse quarters, but only Congress can pass a bill. Congressional constituents—either as individuals or as citizens' groups or associations, labor unions, manufacturers' associations, and chambers of commerce—may avail themselves of the right to provide input into the legislative process. These constituents or groups can often provide the expertise that is lacking on the part of Congress on many complex economic and social issues.

Since laws emanate from Congress, business should be involved at the initial point of contact. America today is composed of a congeries of special interest groups, each with its own constituency. The goals of these interest groups are often directly opposite, for example, prolife versus abortion on demand. There is a tendency toward a divided society and a multiplicity of special interest groups, and money is not likely to be lacking for any interest group with a good-sized bloc of votes. In its self-interest and for its survival as a viable institution, business has to be involved in the political process, because many things that interest groups demand are directly related to business: foolproof consumer products, clean air, and so forth. Congress is where the action begins, and the exercise of political power requires communication. Effective communication between business and Congress has been lacking, at least in the past. Substitutes for first-hand information from business are persons drawn from departments of government, legislative staffs, the academic community, and private consulting firms.

Federal and state legislative bodies are the focal point for business dealings with government, for they make the laws. Thus, it is necessary for business to understand the legislative

process and to establish a personal relationship with congressmen, state legislators, and even city councilmen, for city laws
also can have a considerable impact upon business. It is necessary to be aware of the political point of view, background, and
personality of the person who is the political representative
with whom business has to deal. Staffs are also very important.
There are some 5,000 staff members in the U.S. Senate and
11,000 staff members in the House of Representatives.[5] In California, Florida, Illinois, New York, and other states, legislative
staffs have grown at a geometric rate over the last decade.
Legislative staffs have become an invisible force in lawmaking.
They research, draft, and oversee the implementation of legislative proposals. Legislators have come to depend upon them
for expertise at all stages of the legislative process. Some staff
members have even gained the reputation of being surrogate
legislators and can determine the content of proposed legislation. Knowing the important staff members is a key element in
influencing lawmaking.

Legislators perform most of their legislative work in committees. Former Senator William Hathaway of Maine was correct
when he stated that the committee system is the crux of the
legislative process and is the basis for most legislative action.
Ninety percent of all federal and state legislation is passed in
the form reported by the committee for floor action. Thus,
committees can be a very important access point when it becomes necessary to communicate a business point of view. Timing is of quintessential importance: If the timing is not right,
no idea has much chance of being accepted. A corporation
attempted to add an amendment to the Tax Reform Act of
1976 after it had cleared the House Ways and Means Committee and was scheduled for floor debate. This proved to be an
exercise in futility, for the horse was already out of the barn.
The amendment should have been presented to members of
the House Ways and Means and Senate Finance committees
during, or preferably before, the hearings on tax reform, and
followed up at the time each committee "marked up" the tax
bill for floor action.

Some committees are of particular importance as far as business is concerned. At the federal level of government, there are the Senate Finance Committee and the House Ways and Means Committee, both of which are of paramount importance to business. The House Ways and Means Committee has the power to tax—all revenue-raising bills emanate from this committee. No one thing has more impact upon business than taxation. Former chairman of the House Ways and Means Committee, Congressman Al Ullman of Oregon, and his counterpart on the Senate Finance Committee, Senator Russell Long of Louisiana, were among the most powerful men in Congress. The House and Senate Appropriations committees are also of prime importance to business, for they determine how the money is going to be spent. The House Rules Committee is important because it has control over the order in which bills will be introduced in Congress. It acts as a traffic cop for most legislation and can stamp its own imprint on a piece of legislation. Then there are other committees that can have a considerable impact upon business—the House Committee on Interstate and Foreign Commerce, the Senate and House Judiciary committees, and the Senate and House committees on Banking and Urban Affairs.

In addition to the various committees, there is a wide variety of subcommittees. The framework and parameters of most bills are settled in committees and their subcommittees. Several decades ago, committees became so numerous and unwieldy that it was necessary to reduce their number. Today, there are 22 standing committees in the House of Representatives, less than half the number existing thirty years ago. In the meantime, however, the number of subcommittees has increased to 147, and many of these subcommittees and their chairmen and senior members have assumed considerable influence over the generally smaller slice of legislation they command. These subcommittees have staff members, and chairmen and higher-ranking members also employ staff experts in the subject matter covered by these units. Staff members may play a major role in shaping legislation because their interest and expertise are often deeper than that of the typical legislator, who has to be concerned with a myriad of other issues, constituent matters, and political problems. Reliance on staffs has contributed to the fragmentation of the congressional policy process by strengthening committees and especially subcommittees.[6]

Congress has great political power and an enormous capacity to frustrate the legislative ambitions of any president, as President Carter discovered in the course of his term in office. Congress has become more fractious and less subject to party discipline, and individual legislators have created various enclaves of power. Moreover, there has been an increase in the incumbency effect in congressional elections—the propensity of voters to reelect incumbents—and a concomitant decline in competition.[7] It can be said that Congress has become semi-sovereign, answerable to its various constituencies, but not really to presidential party leadership. Its internal power structure is dispersed, with legislative influence over policy decisions scattered over a large number of members serving on its many subcommittees. Its aggregate decision making is individualistic in the sense that party or committee influence on member voting is not compelling. In this respect, it is totally unlike the parliamentary systems in the United Kingdom, Canada, and elsewhere, where voting is rigidly circumscribed by party lines. This is frustrating to politicians and social reformers who, like Paul on the road to Damascus, have the "received truth," and would like to impose this truth on the rest of society.

A final important factor should be noted as a determinant of congressional policy-making power: Legislation today, in regulatory and nonregulatory fields alike, requires specialized information on the part of policymakers before it can be conceptualized, drafted, and implemented. Policy areas are for the most part highly technical with respect to legal, economic, and political factors. While expert knowledge does not require a Ph.D. in mathematics, engineering, or other basic sciences, or even in the social sciences, it does, on the other hand, demand an intimate acquaintance with the issues that arise in the particular policy areas that are the concern of modern government. This is knowledge that can only be acquired from a variety of areas of specialized competence, including business, before the total picture can be understood.

Executive Branch

The executive branch is the second branch of government. At the federal level of government, the executive branch consists of the president of the United States, his cabinet, and the bureaucracy. The framers of the Constitution created a presidency of limited powers. They wanted a presidential office that would stay clear of parties and factions, enforce the laws passed by Congress, deal with foreign governments, and help the states put down disorders. However, American presidents have been extending the limits of executive power, aided and abetted by Congress and the courts. In times of national emergency, Congress has increased the rule-making discretion of the executive branch. The great growth of the federal government's role has also enlarged the responsibilities of the president. Thus, what the Constitution intended the role of the president to be and what has happened over time are two quite different things. The presidency has increased in power, and White House aides are able to claim that it is the only place in government where it is possible to set and coordinate national priorities. The president is often an access point for well-organized special interest groups who want their views to be given weight in decision-making.

The president of the United States has several responsibilities. First, he is responsible for priority setting and policy formulation. With the trend toward increased centralization in government policymaking, presidents have now become responsible for proposing new federal programs and initiatives in the areas of foreign policy, economic growth and stability, and social welfare. Particularly since the New Deal, presidents have been expected to assume more responsibility in directing economic policy—fighting inflation and preventing depression. The Employment Act of 1946 expanded the responsibility of the president in that the federal government officially assumed the responsibility for promoting maximum employment. Second, the president is responsible for handling national emergencies. "The President shall be Commander-in-Chief of the Army and the Navy of the United States," states Section 2 of

Article II of the Constitution. The military role of the president has increased in importance in the nuclear age. Finally, the president is supposed to be the strongest mobilizer of influence in the American system of power. This is facilitated by ready access to all communications media, which provides immediate contact with the people.

However, the executive branch is by no means limited to the president. There is a host of departments and agencies that come under the jurisdiction of the executive branch. There is the Executive Office of the President, which consists of the Office of Management and Budget, the Council on Environmental Quality, the Council on Wage and Price Stability, the National Security Council, and several other staff units. These units are supposed to coordinate administration policies on matters before the Congress, help the president plan and set priorities, and monitor and evaluate progress toward achieving national objectives. Then there are the various departments of government, the heads of which are appointed by the president and form his cabinet. Then comes the government bureaucracy, which is the administrative arm of the government. It appears to be assuming more and more power at the expense of the legislative and judicial branches. Bureaucracy cannot be dismissed as simply part of the executive branch of government controlled by the president or his cabinet. Its power has increased and it has become an important new political force in the government system, a force that might well become dominant if it is not controlled.

For all practical purposes, the federal bureaucracy and Congress have the greatest impact upon business firms. Congress makes the laws, and the bureaucracies of the many federal agencies enforce them, often interpreting them as they see fit. Business firms come into contact with many bureaucrats representing such agencies as the Internal Revenue Service, the Equal Employment Opportunity Commission, the Environmental Protection Agency, the Consumer Product Safety Commission, and a host of others. Only a small percentage of the bureaucrats work in Washington. The vast majority are employed in regional, field, and local offices scattered throughout the country and around the world. They are not exactly popular with most business firms or, for that matter, with the general public. When one speaks of big government, one is speaking about the bureaucracy. Big government is plainly in disrepute today, occupying a position in public esteem even below that of big business and big labor.[8] It provides an inviting target for politicians and the general public, for few have not been hassled at one time or another in dealing with such agencies as the Internal Revenue Service or the dozens of national regulatory agencies that have been created in recent years.

The bureaucrats work for the various organizational units of the executive branch—the departments, for example, the Department of Commerce—which are subdivided into bureaus and smaller units. Bureaus are the working agencies of the federal government and have definite duties. There are also more than 50 independent agencies embracing over 2,000 bureaus, branches, offices, and other subunits. There is an important difference in the lines of authority between these agencies and the executive branch. They have been created by Congress, and are not organized as part of any of the departments that are the backbone of the executive branch. The Interstate Commerce Commission, the Federal Trade Commission, the Securities and Exchange Commission, and the National Labor Relations Board are examples of such agencies that are very important to the business community. Also, in some states, major administrative agencies are independent of the chief executive. Many state constitutions provide for the election of important administrative officers, such as the attorney general and the state treasurer, and deny the governor the right to remove even department heads except for cause.

On the other hand, some well-known federal agencies are part of the executive branch. For example, both the Food and Drug Administration and the Social Security Administration are part of the Department of Health and Human Services. The Federal Aviation Administration is part of the Department of Transportation. Most local agencies and a majority of state agencies are also organized as part of the executive branch. On a day-to-day basis, this does not make much difference because the agencies operate without interference from the other components of the executive branch, but when agencies are organized within the executive branch, greater potential for direct control does exist. Many major policy decisions within the jurisdictional power of the agencies may be influenced by the chief executive and his staff.

If one views the executive branch as a whole, it becomes evident that most of the departments exercise significant regulatory power. The reasons for locating such power within these departments are similar to those that led to the creation of such independent regulatory commissions as the Interstate Commerce Commission.[9] Regulatory functions are usually performed by separate agencies within departments, and unlike their commission counterparts, they are generally responsible for the regulation of a narrow aspect of private activity, not an entire industry. The Department of Agriculture provides an example of many subordinate groups, with the Commodity Credit Corporation, Commodity Exchange Authority, and Farmers Home Administration engaged in various forms of regulation. Administrative functions, divided into legislative, judicial, and executive categories, are exercised by all types of agencies; however, at the same time, agencies may differ with respect to the reasons for establishment, principal goals, and organizational structures. These factors are largely determined by political forces that lead to the creation of particular agencies and provide a basis for continuing support from constituencies whose interests must be taken into account. Because they must be taken into account, agencies are by definition responsible to their constituencies.

Although the main frame of reference of this chapter is the federal government, it is important to point out the fact that business firms must deal with the legislative, executive, and judicial bodies of the states in which they operate. There are fifty governors and fifty state legislatures. There are many more bureaucrats operating at the state and local levels of government than at the federal level; in fact, federal civilian employment in the past twenty years or so has stayed at the same level and, in comparison with state and local growth rates, has leveled off. States' activities have greatly expanded, their capacity and authority have become more impressive in relation to those of local government, and they have changed their institutional structures so as to be more effective agents of government. States remain an important economic and political arena as far as business is concerned. Although a large portion of the increased scope of state government activities turns out to be promoted and financed by federal funds, there is a sense in which expansion on that basis can be considered a mark of success for the states.[10]

Nevertheless, Washington still is where the action is. The states, like local governments, have become increasingly dependent on federal financial resources. Observers of the federal system of government have become aware of the influence of what is called a "professional-bureaucratic complex" of national, state, and local administrators. Members of this complex, reinforced by elected officials at all levels of government, provide an effective force for the expansion and administration of a number of different programs that have emanated from Washington. Their influence has been increased through the development of various district and intrastate regional agencies more responsive to federal grants than to elected state or local authorities. In this situation, there are some limitations on the policy-making roles of state and local officials who have been elected to assume general responsibilities for their governments.

Judicial Branch

"The first thing we do, let's kill all the lawyers," said Dick the butcher in Henry VI.[11] This Shakespearian sentiment has probably been shared by many people since law became a recognized profession. Nevertheless, the impact of the legal profession upon business is enormous. It can be said, without being facetious, that the vast areas of government regulation of business have created many new jobs for lawyers. There are few business firms without a legal department or at least a legal retainer. Moreover, for decades to come the tone of much federal business regulation will be affected by various decisions handed down by the U.S. Supreme Court. A variety of business issues were covered in the cases heard by the Supreme Court before it adjourned in June 1980. Some of the more important issues heard by the Court are presented in Table 6.1.

Courts, taken together, make up one of the three branches of government; therefore, as is true of the legislative and executive branches, they are generally provided for in the federal and state constitutions.[12] For example, Article III of the U.S. Constitution vests the judicial power of the United States "in one Supreme Court and in such inferior courts as the Congress may from time to time ordain and establish." The system of "inferior" courts has evolved over the years. Today there are federal trial courts in each state, known as district courts, and courts of appeal—one for each of the circuits into which the country is divided. There are also certain specialized courts set up by Congress, including the court of claims, the tax court, and the customs court. There is at least one judicial district, and usually two or more, in each state. The number of judges in each district varies, depending upon the volume of cases. A trial is ordinarily presided over by a single judge, but there are situations in which three-judge district courts are required.

In order for a suit to be filed in the federal district court, it

TABLE 6.1.   Business Issues on the Supreme Court's 1979–80 Calendar [13]

CASE	ISSUE
Finance	
Chiarella v. U.S.	Does the ban on insider stock trading extend to such incidental recipients of information as a printer?
Transamerica Mortgage Advisors v. Lewis	May individual customers sue for damages under the 1940 Investment Advisors Act?
Mobil Oil v. Vermont	May states tax a corporation chartered in another state on earnings from foreign subsidiaries?
Labor	
Carbon Fuel v. UMW	When is a national union financially liable for local wildcat strikes?

TABLE 6.1 *(continued)*

CASE	ISSUE
Nachman Corp. v. Pension Benefits Guaranty Corp.	Is it constitutional to force companies to fund pension plans that were dropped before ERISA took effect?
Antitrust	
McLain v. Real Estate Board of New Orleans	Do federal antitrust laws ban price-fixing on real estate commissions in a local market?
Health and Safety	
AFL-CIO v. American Petroleum Institute	Must OSHA standards be based on a firm estimate of the savings in life or health that would result?
Costle v. Pacific Legal Foundation	Did Congress require the EPA to hold a public meeting on all water discharge permits, even when no one asks for such a hearing?
GTE Sylvania v. Consumers Union	May a consumer group seek through a federal suit product safety data from a government agency after another court has granted a manufacturer's request to enjoin publicizing the information?
Forsham v. Califano	Do outsiders have a legal right to see the raw data generated in federally funded research projects when safety regulations are based on the information?
Civil Rights	
Fullilove v. Kreps	Is it constitutional for the federal government to insist that a set percentage of public works spending go to companies owned by blacks, Hispanics, or other minority-group members?
California Brewers Assn. v. Bryant	Does a union contract defining permanent and temporary workers violate the civil rights laws if it works to the disadvantage of blacks?

must come within one of the classes of cases to which the Constitution extends the federal judicial power: cases between citizens of different states and cases involving questions under federal laws or under the U.S. Constitution. Decisions of the district courts are appealable as a matter of right to the appropriate U.S. court of appeals, and in a few cases, directly to the Supreme Court of the United States. Most of the cases that reach the Supreme Court from the courts of appeals come by way of "certiorari." In such cases, the party who lost the case in the court of appeals is not given the right to appeal to the Supreme Court, but must persuade the Court that it should exercise its discretion and take the case for review because of some special importance it has. In only a small fraction of the cases is the petition for a writ of certiorari granted by the Court.

The fairly standard state court pattern includes the following trial courts. First, there is a court of general jurisdiction, typically called a "district" court or a "circuit" court, to handle all cases not reserved for courts of special jurisdiction and sometimes with a jurisdiction overlapping that of the special courts. Second, there are courts of special jurisdiction to handle specified matters only, for example, probate courts to take proof of the authenticity and validity of wills and supervise the administration of estates. Third, there are small claims courts to handle lawsuits not involving more than a small amount. Finally, all states have an appellate court of last resort, usually called the state supreme court. In most states it is the only court to which appeals may be taken from the trial courts of general jurisdiction. However, some states have intermediate appellate courts whose decisions are final in some cases but may be appealed to the highest court in others. In cases reachable by the judicial power of the United States, as defined in Article III of the Constitution, it may also be possible to obtain review of the decisions of the state courts of last resort by the U.S. Supreme Court.

In the past twenty-five years, the Supreme Court has become a major domestic policymaker in the United States.[14] It is accused by some of its critics and even by some of its own members of being involved in social engineering.[15] The Weber case is an example. Supreme Court decisions have had a substantial impact upon American life. For example, the Court has substantially affected welfare administration by abolishing residency requirements and requiring hearings before benefits are cut off. It has expanded the legal concepts of standing and class action to facilitate a much broader use of litigation as a form of interest group politics. It has given government employees, students, convicts, and illegitimates whole sets of new legal rights, and it has struck at various forms of sexual discrimination. Business is affected by Supreme Court decisions. The Supreme Court has held that inquiries into a prospective employee's criminal record would be racially discriminatory unless the inquiry and the answer it was designed to elicit are somehow directly related to the total assessment of the employee. Policy choices often appear to be made on the basis of the Court's vision of what the good life in the good state should be.

A Guide for Action

The basic rubric of the American political system has been presented in the above discussion of the legislative, executive, and judicial branches of government, but particularly the national government, for that is where most of the decisions affecting business are made. It is now necessary to become more specific in terms of how to deal with those institutions of government that have the most impact upon business. This could be placed under a general heading called "Getting Things Done in Washington." A good starting point is the Congress of the United States, for it has a number of legislative powers, including the power to spend and tax, the power to borrow money, the power to regulate commerce with foreign nations and among the states, and the power to set up the federal courts under the Supreme Court. As a final catchall, the Constitution gave Congress the right "to make all laws which shall be necessary and proper for carrying into execution" the powers set out. A good starting point for how to get things done in Washington is to look at the legislative process in terms of how laws are passed.

7

How Laws
Are Passed

CONGRESSMAN GUY VANDER JAGT OF MICHIGAN once made the statement that "if the free enterprise system is to survive the hostile Washington atmosphere, corporate management must be motivated to act, and must be personally involved in public affairs." [1] Although his statement may be overblown, particularly with respect to the use of the word *hostile,* there is a considerable degree of truth in what he said, and there is reason to be concerned about the increasing encroachment on business decision-making by government bodies. Congress is the prime legislative body in the United States, and it is felt by many observers of the business scene that it is necessary for business to press Congress to promote measures that are of some benefit to it. It is felt, for example, that business is not renewing its plants or buying the modern equipment that is needed.[2] In comparison to West Germany and Japan, productivity in the United States is decreasing. Business must importune Congress to pass measures designed to stimulate capital formation. Of course, it would help if business had more public support; to gain this, it should begin with its own employees.

84

Steps in the Process

Since Congress passes the laws that affect business, it is necessary to understand how laws are passed. Figure 7.1 illustrates how a bill introduced in Congress becomes a law. It is followed by an example of how a law was passed—amendments to the Clean Air Act of 1970. Powerful and competing economic and social interest groups were involved in support or opposition to the amendments: business groups, environmentalists, labor unions, consumers, and health groups. There was much at stake in terms of dollar costs. The interplay of these various groups with Congress is important. It should be noticed that there are appropriate action points when any interest group should press its position on Congress. Timing is of quintessential importance when it comes to influencing a bill. The last thing in the world to do is to wait until a bill has been enacted into law and then try to provide some belated input.

Congress Passes a Law

Any congressman or senator can introduce a bill in Congress, and most do at one time or another. After all, it is one way to make the home folks think they are earning their keep, particularly if there is attendant publicity. But few bills actually become laws. In 1977, for example, 15,386 bills were introduced in the ninety-fifth Congress, 1,483 recorded votes were taken, and 250 bills were actually enacted into law.[3] The probability of a bill becoming a law is small—less than one out of a hundred. But time, intellect, and emotion are devoted to many bills, and a majority consensus must be achieved before a bill is passed into law. This consensus usually results from trade-offs between congressmen—you support this bill, and I will do something for you in return, or quid pro quo is the way to go.[4] Depending upon the importance of the bill, tremendous pressures can be brought against congressmen, particularly those who are on the committees or subcommittees initiating or reporting out the bill. Various special interest groups lobby for or

FIGURE 7.1. How a Bill Becomes a Law. From *Today's Education: Journal of the National Education Association*, 58, no. 3 (March 1969), pp. 28–29. Used with permission.

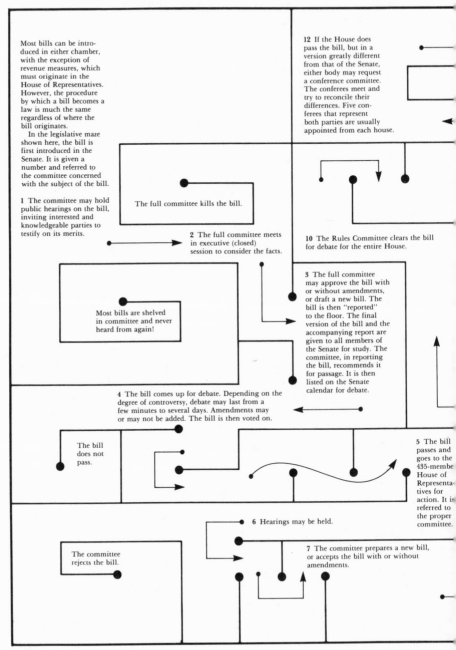

Most bills can be introduced in either chamber, with the exception of revenue measures, which must originate in the House of Representatives. However, the procedure by which a bill becomes a law is much the same regardless of where the bill originates.

In the legislative maze shown here, the bill is first introduced in the Senate. It is given a number and referred to the committee concerned with the subject of the bill.

1 The committee may hold public hearings on the bill, inviting interested and knowledgeable parties to testify on its merits.

The full committee kills the bill.

2 The full committee meets in executive (closed) session to consider the facts.

Most bills are shelved in committee and never heard from again!

4 The bill comes up for debate. Depending on the degree of controversy, debate may last from a few minutes to several days. Amendments may or may not be added. The bill is then voted on.

The bill does not pass.

The committee rejects the bill.

6 Hearings may be held.

12 If the House does pass the bill, but in a version greatly different from that of the Senate, either body may request a conference committee. The conferees meet and try to reconcile their differences. Five conferees that represent both parties are usually appointed from each house.

10 The Rules Committee clears the bill for debate for the entire House.

3 The full committee may approve the bill with or without amendments, or draft a new bill. The bill is then "reported" to the floor. The final version of the bill and the accompanying report are given to all members of the Senate for study. The committee, in reporting the bill, recommends it for passage. It is then listed on the Senate calendar for debate.

5 The bill passes and goes to the 435-member House of Representatives for action. It is referred to the proper committee.

7 The committee prepares a new bill, or accepts the bill with or without amendments.

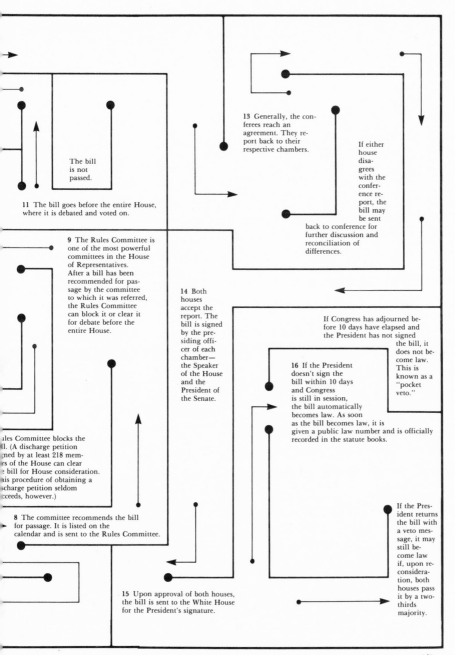

The bill
is not
passed.

11 The bill goes before the entire House, where it is debated and voted on.

9 The Rules Committee is one of the most powerful committees in the House of Representatives. After a bill has been recommended for passage by the committee to which it was referred, the Rules Committee can block it or clear it for debate before the entire House.

...les Committee blocks the ...ll. (A discharge petition ...ned by at least 218 mem-...rs of the House can clear ... bill for House consideration. ...is procedure of obtaining a ...scharge petition seldom ...cceeds, however.)

8 The committee recommends the bill for passage. It is listed on the calendar and is sent to the Rules Committee.

13 Generally, the conferees reach an agreement. They report back to their respective chambers.

If either house disagrees with the conference report, the bill may be sent back to conference for further discussion and reconciliation of differences.

14 Both houses accept the report. The bill is signed by the presiding officer of each chamber— the Speaker of the House and the President of the Senate.

If Congress has adjourned before 10 days have elapsed and the President has not signed the bill, it does not become law. This is known as a "pocket veto."

16 If the President doesn't sign the bill within 10 days and Congress is still in session, the bill automatically becomes law. As soon as the bill becomes law, it is given a public law number and is officially recorded in the statute books.

If the President returns the bill with a veto message, it may still become law if, upon reconsideration, both houses pass it by a two-thirds majority.

15 Upon approval of both houses, the bill is sent to the White House for the President's signature.

against the bill, and each congressman is a target of these groups.

The best way to understand how a bill becomes law is to trace the steps from its incubation to germination.[5] A bill relevant to the interests of business is H.R. 6161, a bill to amend the Clean Air Act of 1970. This act, which sets national standards for air pollution, is the most important of all federal laws governing pollution, and it contains a series of provisions that have a direct impact upon the operations of business firms. The act required that by 1975 new cars be virtually free of pollution and specified that emissions of hydrocarbons and carbon monoxide gases had to be 90 percent lower than levels permissible in 1970. The act also established strict controls for fuel additives and required manufacturers to provide a 50,000-mile warranty on automobile emission control devices. Probably no one piece of legislation has elicited more business complaints than the Clean Air Act, and with considerable justification, for the cost of compliance is enormous.

Introduction of H.R. 6161

H.R. 6161 or, in short, the clean air bill, amended the Clean Air Act of 1970 basically to give the automobile companies more time to comply with auto emission standards. The key issue concerning the bill was whether or not to enforce tougher emission standards. Environmentalists charged that exhaust emissions are the chief source of dirty air; the automobile companies charged that they suffered financially from federal pollution standards and wanted them altered. Both sides marshaled their forces, and in the process strange bedfellows were created. Organized labor joined forces with the managers of the automobile firms to attempt to emasculate the bill. Both labor and management feared economic disruptions in the form of lost jobs and lost sales and opposed the tough emission control standards set forth in the bill. The automobile industry decided to push for a two-year delay in the regulations tightening existing pollution standards. It contended that it lacked the technology to make necessary adjustments and that a delay was necessary, for the 1978 models were subject to emission standards so stringent that a fine of $10,000 per automobile violating the standards would be imposed.

The automobile industry enlisted the support of two congressmen who were dramatically opposite in terms of political philosophy—John Dingell, a liberal Democrat, and James Broyhill, a conservative Republican. Congressman Dingell had a very good reason to support the automobile industry: His congressional district included the corporate headquarters of Ford Motor Company and the homes of most of the workers at the Ford Rouge plant. Since his constituency was comprised primarily of workers in the Ford plant, it was natural for him to be concerned about the impact of the clean air bill on the automobile industry. Broyhill, however, represented a North Carolina district that is more rural in nature and is dominated by furniture plants. The congressman, of course, is a member of the Broyhill family, which is prominent in the furniture industry. Philosophically, Broyhill would be expected to oppose any attempt to increase government regulation of business. However, furniture plants are also subject to the pollution control measures of the Clean Air Act of 1970.

The environmentalist position on the clean air bill of 1977 was as follows: automobiles pollute, and the automobile industry has not solved the problem. The Clean Air Act of 1970 had set specific emission standards that were to be met by 1975. However, by 1977 the timetable of automobile emission standards had been eased three times—twice by the Environmental Protection Agency and once by Congress, after the auto industry contended that it was unable to meet the standards. Proponents of H.R. 6161 were willing to continue to delay emission standards for the 1978 models, but proposed to tighten them after that. Emission standards were to be tightened to 0.41 grams a mile for hydrocarbons from 11.5 grams; carbon monoxide emissions were to be reduced to 3.4 grams in the models of the early 1980s from the then current 15.0 maximum grams per mile. It was these tougher standards that both management and labor opposed—management on the grounds of increased costs resulting from insufficient technology, and labor, represented by the United Auto Workers Union and the AFL-CIO, on the grounds that many jobs would be lost.

The environmentalists were represented by Congressman Paul Rogers, a Florida Democrat from the so-called Gold Coast, which includes West Palm Beach. There are many retirees, much inherited wealth, and little industry in the district Rogers represented. In fact, there cannot be two more diverse districts than those represented by Dingell and Rogers. In 1977 Congressman Rogers was the chairman of the Subcommittee on Health and Government of the Interstate and Foreign Commerce Committee and was a leading advocate for environmental laws. Supporters of the environmental point of view included the American Medical Association, public health groups, and the Consumer Federation of America. Their main approach was that the automobile industry was not moving fast enough to comply with the Clean Air Act, and that a cleaner environment was necessary to preserve the health of all Americans, but particularly children and the aged.

Lobbying Activities

Powerful and competing interest groups were vitally concerned with either passing or defeating the clean air bill. There was overkill on both sides—thousands of jobs would be lost and the economic health of the automobile industry would be in jeopardy versus the counterclaim that Americans would have their health ruined from the noxious fumes of autos. The lobbying for and against the bill involved a confrontation between "jobs" versus "health" and "environment" versus "economy." This confrontation represents a part of an overall conflict between the environment and economic growth. Environmentalists contend that economic growth must be curtailed in the name of ecological sanity. They feel that the level of pollution is a result of economic growth—as real gross national product increases, so does pollution. Supporters of economic growth contend that a constantly increasing real gross national product is necessary to maintain a high level of employment and to improve living standards. Whether they like it or not, and most do not, business firms are caught in the middle of the environment-economic growth conflict.

The initial point of contact for the clean air bill was the

House Subcommittee on Health and the Environment, which was chaired by Congressman Paul Rogers, the leading proponent of the bill. The clean air bill, as is true of any bill, was given a legislative number, H.R. 6161, and assigned to an appropriate subcommittee. It is in committees and subcommittees that the framework and parameters of most bills are developed. More specialized bills, such as the clean air bill, go to a related subcommittee. There are 22 House committees and 147 subcommittees. All have chairmen, members, and a paid staff consisting of persons with expertise in subject matters relevant to the purpose of the committee or subcommittee. Businessmen interested in a particular bill should know who is the chairman of the committee or subcommittee responsible for handling it. They should know who is the ranking minority member. In the Subcommittee on Health and the Environment, it was Congressman Tim Lee Carter of Kentucky (now retired and succeeded by Congressman Dave Stockman of Michigan). It is also desirable to know who the other senior members are. Committee and subcommittee staffs often possess considerable influence, since congressmen may serve on many committees.

Reciprocity is a fact of political life. Congressmen do each other favors, realizing that gains can be made when the "out" party is "in" and vice versa. On important bills, one congressman may support the position of another congressman in return for support on another bill. Congress, but particularly the Democratic party in Congress, is a composite of diverse political philosophies. Straight party voting is rare, and there is little party discipline. In fact, congressmen have become increasingly independent of parties and party labels. Whether this is good or bad is a matter of opinion, but on balance it is probably good because there is a departure from a monolithic party structure. It is harder to discipline congressmen who stray from the party path today because there are so many who do so. In fact, some members make it a political virtue to oppose their leaders.

A number of individuals and groups testified for and against the clean air bill. It is of importance to provide two contrasting points of view on the bill. The first point of view is expressed by Leonard Woodcock, then president of the UAW, who was supported in his testimony against the bill by Howard Paster, national legislative director of the UAW, and David Ragone, dean of the College of Engineering at the University of Michigan. As would be expected, Woodcock talked in terms of the impact that the clean air bill would have on employment in the automobile industry if emission standards were raised. However, the prepared statement of Mr. Woodcock also dealt with the state of technology in the automobile industry and the need for time to develop this technology. In this he was supported by an expert on automobile technology, Dean Ragone. A part of the dialogue at the hearings before the Subcommittee on Health and the Environment is as follows:

> WAXMAN (Henry Waxman is a Democratic congressman from California): Do you [Woodcock] feel that we are putting ourselves in the position of having the automobile industry, the UAW, and those related to the industry, coming in and lobbying each time we get close to that deadline for standards, rather than a sincere commitment to meet those standards?
>
> WOODCOCK: I am not sure that I understand the thrust of your position. Are you suggesting that we abandon our rights to petition Congress?
>
> WAXMAN: When we set standards and deadlines to protect the public health . . . we are leaving ourselves open to have the industry come in and lobby us instead of the industry making a sincere effort to meet those standards. Do you agree with that conclusion?
>
> WOODCOCK: The most threatening one, hydrocarbon, what we are proposing goes to the statutory numbers that are out there now and that, by the way, the industry has been most resistant to.
>
> WAXMAN: I am wondering, from your viewpoint, do you see the industry making a sincere effort to meet the deadlines that we set, or to meet the standards that we asked them to meet for the protection of the public health?
>
> WOODCOCK: They have made considerable progress, and they have made it under pressure. What we propose will keep them under pressure.
>
> BROYHILL (of North Carolina): Do you not think that too stringent standards will have an adverse effect on innovative technologies that are coming on stream at this time? I am

particularly thinking, at this time, of the diesel technology, which is going to be offered more and more on American-made cars. I wonder if you would comment on the effect that these extremes, or more stringent standards that would have to be complied with in the very near future, would have on the possibility of these new technologies, or more innovative technologies being developed?

WOODCOCK: May I have Dean Ragone speak to that, sir?

RAGONE: I believe you are quite right. There are a number of technologies being developed. . . . I believe that it is important to allow these new technologies to be developed. Diesel engines, stratified charges, and there are a number of these that can achieve not only improvements in emissions, but on a national basis a very important goal of fuel economy and petroleum conservation.[6]

Supporters of the clean air bill also had their innings before the subcommittee. Representatives of the American Lung Association talked in terms of health and air quality standards: Failure to attain improvement in air quality and further delays in achieving mandated auto emission standards would have an adverse impact on public health. Environmental groups were represented by the National Audubon Society and the Sierra Club. To some extent, environmental groups possessed an early advantage before the Subcommittee on Health and the Environment, for Congressman Paul Rogers was the sponsor of the clean air bill. He was also the chairman of the subcommittee and was able to control his own panel. However, it is important to point out that hearings before the subcommittee are only the first stage in the legislative process. Although the environmentalists and health groups might carry the day in the subcommittee, the game is not over for the other side. The clean air bill cleared the subcommittee and went before the Committee on Interstate and Foreign Commerce, which is comprised of forty-two members.

The Second Stage

The second stage of the clean air bill now began, for it was before the full Committee on Interstate and Foreign Commerce. The first stage had involved public hearings in which testimony was provided by individuals and groups who were for and against amending the Clean Air Act of 1970. Lobbying on both sides had been involved, with the supporters of amending the Clean Air Act winning the inning. The full committee now had to take action on the bill. At any committee meeting, reports on bills may be made by subcommittees. Amendments may be offered to change the bill itself, and these are subject to acceptance or rejection by the House of Representatives. A vote of committee members is taken to either report a bill favorably to the House, with or without amendments, or to table it. The latter has the effect of killing a bill. Committee action then is a key stage in the success or lack of it for a bill, and this was where both supporters and opponents of the clean air bill stepped up their lobbying activities.

Lobbying has come to have a pejorative connotation. It conjures up images of political operators who dispense money and call girls to politicians in return for favors. In fact, the famous political cartoonist of the last century, Thomas Nast, caricatured lobbyists as cigar-smoking, pot-bellied men in bowler hats who carried money bags around to buy politicians. This caricature created an image that is still somewhat prevalent today. However, lobbyists of today do not fit the accepted image. They have to possess a degree of savoir faire and knowledge of the subject to represent their point of view or the view of their clients, if they represent an association. Lobbyists may be former congressmen who have expertise and contacts in a particular area, and who have decided to remain in Washington to work for a particular business or consumer association.

The amendments to the Clean Air Act, as incorporated in H.R. 6161—the Rogers bill—faced their first major hurdle before the full committee. Congressmen Dingell and Broyhill, opponents of the bill, had drafted their own set of amendments, which they had incorporated into a separate bill—H.R. 4444, but this was incidental to the main action. Lobbying efforts for and against the Rogers bill increased in intensity. Labor union lobbyists, who were against the bill, concentrated on Democratic members of the committee, stressing loss of jobs in their districts. Business lobbyists concentrated on Republican members of the committee. On the other side, lobbyists and consumer groups supporting H.R. 6161 also contacted committee members. Those members who were for or against the bill also attempted to persuade uncommitted members. President Carter came down on the side of Congressman Rogers and the environmentalists, committing the power and prestige of the White House in support of the clean air bill. Normally, the president of the United States can exert considerable pressure on legislators, particularly those of his own party, through patronage and public projects that benefit their home districts.

A crucial stage was reached in the consideration of the bill, with neither side confident of a majority of votes. Several congressmen were still undecided as to how they would vote. A skilled tactician in legislative procedures can utilize rules to maximum advantage. Thus, both sides delayed the vote in order to marshall additional support. Lobbying efforts increased in intensity, and committee members used personal persuasion upon the uncommitted. Members also used the "spit in the wind" approach to test home district sentiment. Hometown newspapers can provide a clue to which way the wind is blowing. National newspapers, but particularly syndicated columnists who are widely read, are a source of contact. A syndicated columnist can make a politician look good or bad to the home folks. Above all, the home constituency must be taken into account, for they are vital to any politician's well-being. If the issue is jobs versus a cleaner environment, they are likely to opt for the jobs.

Voting then took place on the clean air bill, specifically on whether or not to dilute its emission standards, which was the objective of Dingell and Broyhill. The voting ended up in a 21–21 tie, with committee chairman Harley Staggers absent. The tie vote constituted a defeat for the supporters of diluting the clean air bill and a victory for its proponents. A majority vote for the Dingell-Broyhill proposals was not obtained, and the clean air bill was then reported to the full House of Representatives. When any committee votes to report a bill favorably to the House, one of its members is designated to write the full committee report. The report describes the purpose and scope of the bill and the reasons for its recommended approval. A section-by-section analysis is set forth in detail, explaining precisely what each section is designed to accomplish. Amendments may be added to any bill. Currently, every report on a bill by a committee must have an impact statement concerning the potential effect of the bill's enactment on prices and costs to the national economy.

The Third Stage

The Rogers bill reached the House of Representatives. This is where the chips are down as far as lobbying activities are concerned. There are 435 House members involved in deciding whether or not a bill will become a law. There is little rigidity or discipline at the national legislative level, and coalitions of Republicans and Democrats form to support or oppose almost every issue. Lobbyists have to contact as many House members as possible; these contacts become more important as a bill nears House action. Various interest groups come to Washington to lobby for and against the bill. Often direct mail from constituents and other interested parties is used to demonstrate a show of strength to convince House members to take desired stands. It might be added that direct mail can be a rather effective device in persuading a congressman to consider a particular point of view.

The Rules Committee of the House of Representatives has jurisdiction over the order of business of the House. A bill can be considered immediately by the Rules Committee or postponed for future consideration. The clean air bill passed through the Rules Committee and then went to the House floor for a vote. Lobbying activities by all groups increased in intensity, for the great majority of House members were not familiar with this piece of legislation. Each has to be contacted, and personal ties with any member are of prime importance. Most members were contacted by a variety of interest groups before the clean air bill went to the floor of the House for discussion and debate. Any member may offer an amendment, and members recognized by the chairman of the House are allowed five minutes to speak for or against it. An amendment is a good way to emasculate the original intent of a bill. On an amendment of any importance, a roll-call vote is usually demanded.

In the case of the clean air bill, an amendment was submitted by Congressman Richardson Preyer of North Carolina. The amendment represented a compromise on the Rogers position, softening the emission control standards as set forth in his bill. The Dingell-Broyhill forces convinced other members of the House that the clean air bill was too hard on the automobile industry. Many congressmen were convinced that to pass the bill would be harder on the car dealers in their districts who lobbied against it than on the environmentalists who were for it. The Preyer amendment, which represented a compromise between the Rogers and Dingell-Broyhill positions, was voted on and defeated by a vote of 190 to 202. The Dingell-Broyhill position that stricter emission requirements not be imposed upon the automobile industry had won, at least temporarily, in the House of Representatives. However, this was not the final stage in the evolution of the bill.

Final Stage

The final stage in the legislative process involved the U.S. Senate. Senate committees give a bill the same detailed consideration it receives in the House and may report it with or without amendments or table it. The Senate is subject to the same lobbying pressures as is the House, but Senators are a little more immune since they come up for reelection every six years rather than every two. Senators may introduce bills, and committees report bills just as in the House. All committee hearings, including those to conduct hearings, must be open to the public. When a bill clears a Senate committee, it is then reported to the full Senate. If the bill is of a noncontroversial nature and there is no objection, the Senate may pass it with only a brief explanation of its purpose and effect and little or no debate. A bill may be amended by any senator, and a simple majority vote is sufficient to carry an amendment or to pass a bill. When there is substantial disagreement between the Senate and House, a joint conference can be called to resolve the differences.

The clean air bill was controversial in that it involved an environment versus economy issue that enlisted the interests of diverse political groups. Although the clean air bill sponsored by Congressman Rogers won in the House, it had to be considered by the Senate. The end result was a compromise between House and Senate conferees. The Senate adopted tougher automobile emission standards than those acceptable to the House. Therefore, the House and Senate appointed a group of conferees to represent each body in conference. From the House side, the main protagonists, Rogers, Dingell, and Broyhill, were included in conference. The result was a compromise that pleased neither the environmentalists nor the automobile industry and the UAW. But the compromise illustrated the political axiom that politics is the art of the possible.

Businessmen can learn many lessons from this example of how a law is passed. There was an interplay of many forces representing the divisions in American society. If there had been no business inputs into the clean air bill, the result probably would have been more one-sided in favor of the environmental position than it actually was. The stakes were very high, and billions of dollars rode on the decision. The days are gone when businessmen can limit their interest in government to gripes about it at the weekly meeting of the Rotary Club. Businessmen of today have to have more economic and political savoir faire than their counterparts of a decade ago. There are competing interests in all political and philosophical debates, and lawmakers pay attention to whichever interest carries the most weight or makes the most noise. Business must know how the whole legislative process works and then play by the rules of the game. It is possible to lose in the first round, as the business-labor forces did on the Rogers bill, but eventually end up winning the fight, or at least not losing it when a bill eventually becomes a law.

8

Dealing with Legislators

AN OBSERVATION OFTEN HEARD from businessmen is that this state legislature, that city council, or Congress is about to pass a rash of antibusiness bills. In order to have a greater input into bills that affect their interests, business firms are recognizing the need to put their best foot forward. But often their attempts fall woefully short, illustrating that there are right and wrong ways to influence legislative decisions. Cases in point involved the 1976 congressional tax reform legislation, which quite obviously had a major impact upon business. The rationale for tax reform was to amend certain provisions of the tax code that were alleged to be loopholes for both corporations and individuals. Hundreds of corporations and trade associations attempted to influence the formulation of the new tax legislation, but most had either no discernible plan for affecting its outcome, or worse, misdirected their influence. A few corporations and trade associations performed well, thus protecting themselves from increased taxes and other indirect costs of tax change. The following three examples illustrate the right and wrong ways of handling the tax reform legislation.

Industry A responded quickly to an incipient congressional

attempt to eliminate certain tax incentives designed to stimulate investment. To influence the drafting of the tax reform bill by the House Ways and Means Committee, a survey was made by the industry's trade association to determine the impact of the reform on employment in the home district of each committee member. The results were conveyed to each member by home district firms of Industry A. Trade association lobbyists also contacted professional staff members working for each member. Similar procedures were also used for the Senate Finance Committee, the Senate counterpart to Ways and Means. In addition to direct trade association contact with members of both committees and their staffs, a letter writing campaign was organized. Each member received letters from his district or state arguing against the tax reform in terms of jobs and dollars lost. Telephone calls from members' friends, who were usually constituents, were made to their Washington offices.

After the preliminary work was done, trade association lobbyists kept tabs on the responses of committee members and their staffs. When commitments by representatives and senators to vote against the particular reforms that affected Industry A were not received, another round of personal visits to the uncommitted was arranged by the lobbyists. More phone calls and letters from home districts and states were also made. The key ingredient in this second effort involved the use of tax impact information by the trade association. The result of the lobbying effort by the trade association and its members was a success in forestalling changes in the tax code that would have been inimical to the interest of Industry A.

Firm B, a major corporation with headquarters in Chicago, also attempted to influence certain components of the tax reform bill. Little direction was given to its business representative in Washington as he began to make known the company's position. He was told to make important contacts but was given little information concerning the impact of the various tax reform proposals on the company. The representative had had little previous contact with members of the Ways and Means and Finance Committees and their staffs. Initial visits to the committees were made well after they had begun consideration of the various tax reform proposals. When presentations were made by the representative to the staff and members of the committees, they lacked substance and contained little reference to the particular impact of the tax proposals on Firm B.

The firm continued to misdirect its efforts when, at a key stage in the consideration of the tax reform legislation, its president decided to fly to Washington to influence members of the Senate Finance Committee. The decision was made less than a day prior to his Washington arrival. The Washington representative of the firm hurriedly telephoned members of the committee to arrange appointments for the president, but he was only able to arrange an appointment with one senator, who was already committed to voting for tax amendments favorable to Firm B. The president met with this senator and also with four staff members who worked for Finance Committee senators who were generally favorable to business interests. His efforts were obviously a waste of time; unfortunately, however, the blame was placed on the Washington representative by the president, who said to him, "Don't ever do this to me again." It was poor planning on the part of Firm B that cost it any influence on the tax committees. It had not coordinated its efforts with its trade association, its Washington representative, or, for that matter, with its plant managers, financial personnel, and stockholders. As a result, measures were passed that had an adverse impact on Firm B.

Firm C, a Texas-based corporation, represents a classic example of the wrong way to influence congressional legislation. The president of this company attempted to use monetary leverage to benefit the company during consideration of tax reform proposals by the Finance and Ways and Means Committees. Substantial campaign contributions had been made to buy members of both committees. A member of the Ways and Means Committee offered an amendment to the tax reform proposals that would have provided substantial tax savings to Firm C. The amendment was adopted and included in legislation sent to the House Rules Committee, which scheduled it for consideration by the full House membership. The amendment, along with other tax reform proposals, was accepted and sent to the Senate for consideration by the Finance Committee. The Finance Committee held extensive hearings that reviewed each component of the tax reform bill. Firm C's amendment was not questioned during these hearings.

As the bill was being "marked up" by the committee, a reporter for an internationally known newspaper wrote an article disclosing the nature of the amendment.[1] This article caused considerable consternation among the members of the Finance Committee. Attention was immediately given to the amendment by the committee members and their staffs. The political implications were weighed, and the day after the article appeared the amendment was deleted from the tax reform bill. The use of monetary leverage by Firm C not only redounded to its disadvantage, but also tended to undermine attempts by other firms to legitimately influence congressional decisions.

Knowing the Right People

As mentioned in the preceding chapter, federal and state legislative bodies make the laws that affect business. Therefore, it is not only necessary to understand the legislative process, but it is also desirable to establish a personal relationship with congressmen, state legislators, and even city councilmen, for city laws also have an impact upon business. If nothing else, business should be aware of the political points of view, backgrounds, and personalities of those persons who are the political representatives with whom it has to deal. This is relatively easy to do, for there are several sources of available information. Most daily newspapers provide information pertaining to how congressmen and state legislators have voted or plan to vote on a particular bill. *Congressional Quarterly*, which is published weekly, provides a summary of how each representative and senator voted on specific bills. It also provides ratings of congressmen by various liberal and conservative groups. Trade associations also provide information on the background and voting predilections of legislators. The *Congressional Directory* is an excellent source of information, providing not only information about each representative and senator, but also the names of their main assistants and a list of House and Senate committees and subcommittees.

However, from the standpoint of political contacts, it is not sufficient to know the legislator. The typical congressman spends about two hours per working day in the office; most of his time is spent in committee meetings or voting on bills. The everyday operations of the office depend on the administrative and legislative assistants and the secretaries, who handle the voluminous day-to-day complaints and requests of constituents. The administrative assistant runs the office, while legislative assistants advise the legislator on various bills. It is important to know at least the names of the administrative and legislative assistants, for they have direct contact with the legislator and can provide valuable input. In situations involving a government regulatory agency, the administrative assistant is probably the person who will contact the agency, not the legislator. Where bills that affect business are involved, the appropriate person to contact is the legislative assistant, for it is his or her responsibility to provide data to the legislator concerning the bills.

It has been mentioned previously that Congress is comprised of a number of committees and subcommittees that do the basic legislative work. These committees have been called the "little legislatures," because they do the work on the bills introduced in Congress. The standing committees have great power, for all bills introduced in the House of Representatives are referred to them. They can defeat bills, pigeonhole them for weeks, amend them, or speed them on their way. A committee reports out favorably only a small fraction of all the bills that come to it. The committees and subcommittees are separate little centers of power, with rules, patterns of action, and internal processes of their own. All have staffs, creating a legislative bureaucracy that has doubled in numbers since 1970. These staffs are supposed to draft and monitor legislation in the areas over which the committees and subcommittees have jurisdiction. They are directly involved in shaping legislation in such critical and highly technical areas as energy and the environment.

Knowing important staff members is a key element in influencing lawmaking. The typical congressman serves on a number of committees and subcommittees. For example, a senator normally serves on three committees and often as many as eight subcommittees. Although assignment to committees is usually linked to the interest of the particular congressman, it is impossible for anyone to have the expertise to be effective on a number of committees. Congress has come to depend increasingly upon senior committee staff members to provide this expertise. These staff members have gained the reputation of being surrogate legislators, and they have an influence on the legislative content of any bill. Senator Ernest Hollings of South Carolina made the statement that "it has grown to the point where senators never actually sit down and exchange ideas and learn from the experience of others." [2] He was, of course, referring to the reliance upon committee staffs. From a business standpoint, it is necessary to know who the senior staff members are on the committees and subcommittees that have the most impact upon business operations.

How to Communicate Effectively with the Lawmakers

Representation of a business point of view to legislators and their staff members can take a number of forms, including telephone calls, letters, personal visits, legislative briefings, testifying before committees, and lobbying through trade associations. About the only approach that is not particularly effective is the telephone call. The Bell Telephone commercial that says "Reach out and touch someone" doesn't necessarily work when it comes to contacting congressmen, for they are rarely in their offices to receive calls. Of necessity, incoming calls are screened in order of priority, and only a few are actually returned. If a telephone call is used, it is preferable to call the administrative assistant. However, there is only so much that can be said over a telephone. It is better to rely on letters, personal visits, and other forms of contact.

Letter Writing

The average congressman receives hundreds of letters, telephone calls, and telegrams each day and is able to read and acknowledge only a small fraction of these. There are other tasks to perform, and response has to be turned over to staff members. Letters are typed overnight on programmed typewriters and signed by a signature machine. It is thus legitimate to question the efficacy of a full-page ad placed by Warner and Swasey in *Business Week.* The pitch of the ad is "Write your congressman and tell him that America must live within its means. By all means, let him know that there isn't much time." Will writing a congressman make a difference? The answer is yes, provided that certain rules are followed. Communications that are likely to be disregarded include:

1. Letters written by persons whom the congressman does not represent
2. Letters that urge the congressman to take a stand on an issue over which he has no jurisdiction
3. Letters that are mass-produced, mimeographed, or photocopied
4. Short letters, telegrams, or coupons clipped from a union or trade association magazine that ask a legislator to vote for or against a particular bill
5. A thank-you letter congratulating the legislator for his or her vote for or against a particular bill
6. A letter urging the legislator to support or oppose a proposal made by the president

There is, however, a correct approach to sending letters and other forms of communication. Legislators and their staffs will be much more likely to pay attention to:

1. Letters or telegrams requesting assistance for a constituent
2. Letters that provide important data or analysis relevant to legislation that is to be introduced
3. Letters that provide a detailed explanation of a statutory inequality
4. Letters written on a first-name basis (it helps to know the legislator personally, or at least his or her administrative assistant)

The old adage "A spoonful of honey will attract more flies than a jar of vinegar" is relevant when it comes to writing letters to congressmen. There is a right way and a wrong way to write letters. Acrimonious letters are obviously not going to get a response. There is a story that involves the former senator from Ohio, Stephen Young, who was pretty much a maverick in politics. A constituent wrote him a rather vitriolic and personal letter. The senator wrote back to the constituent, saying, "Dear Mr.————: I think that you should be aware of the fact that some damn fool is signing his name to your letters." Senator Young expressed a feeling that many legislators would like to express but are too circumspect to do so. It might be added that most letters of this type would be ignored.

It is also rather pointless to write congressmen concerning issues over which they have no control. Former Virginia congressman Richard H. Poff received letters and phone calls from farmers in his district holding him personally responsible for daylight savings time. It seems that changes in the time from regular to daylight had a traumatic effect upon the egg-laying habits of the farmers' chickens and the milk-producing habits of the cows. The roosters didn't know when to crow, the chickens didn't know when to lay eggs, and the cows didn't know when to give milk, or so the farmers claimed. Since farmers were an integral part of the congressman's district and provided a base of support, he couldn't afford to ignore them. His appropriate response was to sympathize with them, blame whoever thought up the idea of daylight savings time, and promise to look into the situation. Apparently, the farmers were satisfied with his response.

An example of a good letter is one that was submitted by the director of corporate taxes for the Whirlpool Corporation to Senator Dale Bumpers of Arkansas.[3] The issue was the investment tax credit, which can have a direct impact on private capital investment. In fact, the tax credit for investment in business equipment was the largest item in the business investment category included in the 1977 federal budget.

> A one-year ITC of 10 percent or 12 percent would have very little real impact on Whirlpool's spending plans. It would be an ineffective incentive to increase expenditures due to our reliance on long-range planning and the unusually long lead times involved between placing an

order and receipt and installation of equipment. Depending upon the nature and complexity of the equipment, this period is normally over a year. Our company planners cannot make judgments based on estimates of what the Congress is likely to do from one year to the next. We have, however, always considered ITC in our capital planning, because it means dollars.

The November 16, 1974 issue of *Business Week* contained an article on the ITC which carried a chart illustrating the impact of the ITC on capital investment. The correlation between machinery orders and the ITC was also demonstrated in a Senate Finance Committee report on the Revenue Act of 1971. A chart on the report illustrating the fluctuations in machine tool orders related to the status of the ITC is attached.

The ITC can only be a significant incentive to capital expenditure increases if it is substantial—in the 10 to 12 percent range—and permanent. In this regard, I was particularly interested in Senator Kennedy's proposed amendment to increase the ITC to 15 percent permanently for "net new investment." The Senator defines this as "the amount of the investment that exceeds a firm's average investment over the preceding three years." A law of this type could have a decided impact on Whirlpool's capital expenditure plans.

This letter is well documented and makes clear the impact of the tax proposal upon Whirlpool's operations. Reference is made in the letter to the fact that a close political ally of Senator Bumpers has supported an even greater ITC. The one thing that is lacking is a direct tie-in with Whirlpool's facilities in Arkansas, a factor of obvious importance to the senator. This tie-in should have included the number of jobs a permanent investment tax credit would create at Whirlpool's operations in Arkansas and the state tax revenue these jobs would create over a period of time.

"Brevity is the soul of wit," said Polonius to Hamlet's mother. "Therefore, I will be brief: your son is mad." [4] This is called getting to the point in a hurry. In writing a letter to a congress-man, it is desirable to limit the contents to one page. The salient points should be stated as concisely as possible. Most letters are routine in their requests, usually asking for assistance with social security or veterans' problems. They are handled by staff personnel who are responsible for this type of assistance. Letters on specific issues will come to the attention of the congressman, but they must be read in a short period of time. It is also not a bad idea to follow up the letter with a telephone call to the administrative assistant or legislative aide. This keeps the issue in front of the congressman.

Personal Visits

The personal visit has the advantage of establishing direct contact with legislators and their staffs. It is better to meet with legislators or their staffs in their home districts rather than in their capital offices. For one thing, there are fewer distractions and interruptions—anyone who has visited a congressman in his Washington office can testify to that. Second, they know for sure that you are a constituent and are more likely to give you their attention. Finally, it is usually easier and less expensive for businessmen to meet in the home office than to go to Washington or to a state capital. If it is necessary to meet in the capital office, an appointment should be made in advance. Although Oscar Wilde once said, "Punctuality is the thief of time," [5] it is important to be punctual for an appointment. Be prepared to answer questions and to leave within the prescribed time period. It is also a good idea to leave some prepared materials stating your views on the issues in question for the legislator to read.

Trade associations, unions, and special interest groups can effectively utilize the personal visit to accomplish their desired goals. For example, the National Association of Postal Supervisors claims that over 400 visits made to Congress by members attending a legislative conference in Washington helped to pass a bill favorable to postal interests. Appointments were made in advance, and all the necessary social amenities were observed. One congressman made the comment, "I want to say that your members are always welcome in my office at any time; what a difference from some of the groups I have to see! I am for you and your bill." [6] This formula has also worked for business groups.

Legislative Briefings

Legislative briefings are a variant of the personal visit, and they are being used by corporations, trade associations, and unions to present specific points of view to legislators and their staffs. The Whirlpool Corporation presented its views to various congressmen at a so-called federal legislator's briefing. A video and sound presentation was supplemented by the use of a briefing book, which contained key issues of importance to the company—business credibility, product safety, consumerism, and tax policies, in particular the investment credit. Included in the legislative briefing was a copy of the letter to Senator Dale Bumpers stating the position of Whirlpool on the investment tax credit. The main merit of legislative briefings is that a corporation or trade association can reach more people and cover more subjects in a relatively short period of time.

A case in point is the annual legislative briefing held in Washington by the Associated Industries of Alabama (AIA), to which the eight representatives and two senators representing the state are invited. The last briefing was held at the L'Enfant Plaza Hotel, which is a short distance from the House and Senate office buildings. A number of subjects of concern of Alabama business firms were on the agenda. In the area of antitrust, opposition was expressed by the trade association to the Kennedy-Rodino bill (S. 300, H.R. 2060), which would drastically change the existing antitrust laws so as to allow "indirect purchasers" of goods and services to sue for triple damages and also to make it very difficult for "direct purchasers" to recover for antitrust violations.[7] Under existing antitrust laws, only "direct purchasers" may recover triple damages from a seller who overcharges them in violation of the laws.[8] AIA took the position that if "indirect purchasers" could bring triple damage suits, including class action suits on the part of consumers, there would be no real benefit to consumers. Instead, the real winners would be the lawyers who would bring or defend endless and enormously costly legal actions.

The export policies of the U.S. government were also of concern to the Associated Industries of Alabama. It complained that federal regulation of business has a deleterious effect upon international trade, arguing that red tape and paperwork requirements imposed by the government reduce business incentives to develop, produce, and market internationally competitive products. It felt that all federal regulatory agencies should be required to prepare economic impact statements, with provisions for public comments, before issuing new regulations. Any new regulatory standard should be limited to those instances in which the agency can demonstrate that the benefits clearly exceed the costs imposed. The trade association also felt that foreign business firms are given a competitive advantage over American firms through various kinds of foreign government financial support. When U.S. exporters compete against European and Japanese firms in third-world markets, the support given by the Export-Import Bank and the Foreign Credit Insurance Corporation tends to be noncompetitive in terms of required downpayment, exporter retention, duration of financing, and interest rates. Complaints were also registered about alleged "dumping" practices of the Japanese and about the Foreign Corrupt Practices Act. It was recommended that the act be amended to provide American business greater flexibility in meeting competition in foreign markets.

Other issues of concern to the AIA included unemployment compensation, rules of the Occupational Safety and Health Administration (OSHA), capital formation and tax incentives, national health insurance, and air and water quality laws. There was concern that the federal government would change the unemployment compensation system from a job insurance program to a welfare program, with increased federal control. Complaints were registered about the paperwork required by OSHA and its conflicting rules and regulations. Dissatisfaction was expressed over everything from enforcement to policymaking procedures of OSHA. It might be added that probably more business firms complain about OSHA than any other federal agency. The AIA stressed the need for new tax incentives designed to stimulate capital formation and opposed the adoption of a national health insurance program. Environmental laws were also of concern to the AIA, particularly the Clean Air Act Amendments of 1977. These amendments, according to the AIA, represent one of the most draconian pieces of environmental legislation ever passed. The belief was expressed that more attention should be given to achieving a balance between economic growth, energy goals, and the environment and that emphasis should be placed on the use of cost-benefit analysis in the area of environmental protection.

Each member of the Alabama congressional delegation was given a notebook outlining the positions of AIA on a range of issues, including those mentioned above. The notebook was indexed by subject matter, making it easy for a congressman to turn to a particular subject. The materials presented were well researched and documented. A list of business firms represented by AIA was included in the notebook. A cover letter was used in the notebook to thank each member of the Alabama congressional delegation for attending the meeting and for listening to the views of the AIA concerning the protection of the free enterprise system. A personal touch was used by giving each congressman a notebook with his name on it.

Testifying before Committees

Mark Twain once said, "Thunder is impressive, but lightning does the work." [9] Although it is important to communicate with individual congressmen, committees are usually the key access point when any group wants to express its point of view. Most legislation is passed in the form reported by a committee for floor action, and committee staff members have considerable clout when it comes to drafting legislation. Testimony before committees is an effective way to communicate with those persons who make the laws.

Testimony before a committee is not limited to an elite group of high-ranking corporate officers and labor union officials. A legislator, if he or she wishes, can convene a hearing and take testimony from anyone. Sometimes it is necessary to seek different points of view to get assistance on diverse issues. There is no reason for anyone to be intimidated by the aura that some people attach to Congress, for congressmen need to be educated the same as everyone else. Ideally, testimony should be presented to a committee or subcommittee at least a few days in advance of the hearings. Questions can also be provided to anticipate important points that committee members might raise. Above all, do not read the testimony verbatim. Like a dull sermon, nothing can be more soporific. Summarize the major points and use visual aids where feasible. Leave time for questions to be raised by committee and staff members, for, contrary to popular view, they are interested in learning about business problems. Testifying is usually a one-shot deal, so it is necessary to make the most of the allotted time.

It is also considered good practice to ask associates to role play the hearings with you before you testify. They should ask you tough questions in anticipation of what might very well be asked by someone in opposition to a business position. Many corporations have videotaping facilities that can be used to hone your presentation. In any case, at the minimum you should tape-record your session with associates and listen to it for clues that will improve your performance at the hearings. Keep in mind that you will be allowed to testify only once, and it will be under trying conditions. If you want to get your point across, it does not matter how informed you are on the subject, you must be well informed about the total legislative process. It is also possible to make a follow-up input into the "markup sessions." Many special interest groups have the time and money to do the follow-up, and if they oppose you, your trip to Washington may turn out to be a sight-seeing trip no matter how correct you are.

An example of testifying before a committee or subcommittee is provided in the statement of Frank Samford, chairman of the board of Liberty National Life Insurance Company, who appeared at the hearings held by the Senate Judiciary Subcommittee on Antitrust and Monopoly.[10] The issue concerned criticisms of home service life insurance. The Federal Trade Commission had published a document called "Policy Planning Issues Paper: Life Insurance Sold to the Poor," which was critical of certain aspects of the insurance industry. The document suggested, among other things, that insurance companies derive a disproportionately high profit from industrial life insurance as compared to ordinary life insurance.[11] Insurance agents selling industrial life insurance were accused of making disproportionately high commissions from selling policies to poor people. Insurance companies allegedly encouraged the sale of industrial insurance because of the high lapse rates on the part of the poor. Finally, the Federal Trade Commission document asserted that small insurance policies are more expensive than larger policies, and policies where premiums are collected by the agent are more expensive than those where premiums are paid directly to the insurance company—both situations imposing financial hardships on poor persons.[12]

Mr. Samford presented the views of the Liberty National Life Insurance Company, beginning with the mechanics of life insurance. Topics discussed included the economics of industrial insurance and the proportion of premiums allocated to expenses. A criticism of industrial life insurance is that its regulation is less strict than the regulation of ordinary life insurance and that the policy provisions permitted in industrial life insurance are less favorable to the insured. This criticism was disputed by Mr. Samford, who also took exception to the Federal Trade Commission's claim that industrial insurance is much more profitable than ordinary life insurance. Testimony before the Subcommittee on Antitrust and Monopoly at least provided the opportunity for a representative of the insurance industry to present a particular viewpoint on a complex subject. In addition to his personal testimony, Mr. Samford provided members and staff of the subcommittee with bound copies of his overall statements.

The Press Conference

A press conference is one way to express a point of view presented by the president or any senior officer of a company. It can be used to get across a business message to the Washington community. However, it is important to know the press and to schedule the press conference so that it doesn't conflict with key hearings and other activities. The press conference should be held at a convenient place in downtown Washington or on Capitol Hill. It is also important to provide summary information sheets concerning the issues discussed and to give the press time to raise questions. Keep the press conference short and to the point, and hold a reception after the conference, for many persons will come to a reception but not to a press conference alone. If possible, use visual aids, charts, and graphs to illustrate a point, and accommodate requests for information and assistance. On the don't side: Don't attack without presenting an alternative proposal, and don't forget to include industry and trade association supporters in the conference.

9

How to Deal with Congressional Staffs

Congressional staffs have been called "the invisible force in American lawmaking" by one observer of the Washington scene, while another observer has stated that "congressional staffs are no less essential to the care, feeding, and orderly operation of Congress than Merlin was to King Arthur or Cardinal Richelieu was to Louis XIII." [1] Both statements are essentially correct. Similarly, former Senator Robert Morgan of North Carolina made the statement that "this country is basically run by the legislative staffs of the members of the Senate and the House of Representatives." [2] Staff, as he uses the word, is the currency of the Congress, both in personal offices and in the congressional committees and subcommittees. There is no question that Congress depends upon staff personnel, for in all legislation they are the ones who lay out the options. Congressional power is bought with staff resources, for while senators and representatives debate, vote, hold hearings, and make public appearances, it is the staff members who are setting up the hearings, writing speeches, answering mail, turning ideas into legislation, and overseeing the implementation of laws. In other words, they do most of the work on Capitol Hill.

115

Although most people have heard about congressional staffs, few know what they actually do. They remain on anonymous group, usually not mentioned in a high school civics course or in an American government textbook used by college freshmen. But there are 20,000 staffers to 535 members of Congress —a ratio of 37 to 1. The number of personal and committee staff employees has increased from just over a hundred in the latter part of the nineteenth century to 20,000 today.[3] The average Senate personal office staff exceeds 40, and its House counterpart averages around 14 persons. Committee and subcommittee employees total over 3,000, with approximately 2,000 employed by the House and 12,000 employed by the Senate. Twenty years ago Congress got by with $128 million budget and 6,400 staffers. Since that time, the number of staff personnel has tripled, and the cost of staffing has increased to an estimated $1.2 billion.[4] This does not include the cost of converting old hotels and apartment buildings near the Capitol into office space to hold this staff, nor does it include the $137 million being spent to construct a third Senate office building to provide still more room.

There are several reasons for this expansion in congressional staff personnel. First, there is the rivalry between the executive and legislative branches of government. In part, this rivalry began during the Vietnam War, when Congress began to doubt what it was being told by the White House. Some congressmen began to hire their own staffs of experts to delve into controversial issues. After years of wrangling with the White House over spending priorities, in 1974 the House and Senate set up their own budget committees, each with a staff of 80. For good measure, a separate Congressional Budget Office, with 200 staff members, was also created. Second, Republicans also made demands for their own minority staffs for each committee and subcommittee, and some 1,500 additional staff workers were added during the 1970s. Finally, the complexity of drafting and monitoring legislation in such highly technical areas as energy and the environment mandated an increase in the number of skilled, top-salaried employees. It is among these professional staffers—those directly involved in shaping legislation —that hiring has become most dramatic. The number of top-salaried employees has doubled in the Senate and quintupled in the House in the past twenty years.[5]

Functions of Personal Staffs

Personal staffs of House members include both district and Washington staffs. Most members have at least one district office, and it is not uncommon for a second or third office to be established. Congressman William C. Wampler of Virginia, ranking Republican on the House Agricultural Committee, represents a district that is geographically larger than the state of Connecticut. He maintains three offices in his mountainous and largely rural district. Casework and social security problems are usually handled in these offices. In the Washington office, Wampler's staff includes an administrative assistant, a legislative assistant, a press secretary, a receptionist, a personal secretary, and caseworkers. This is about par for most members of the House of Representatives. The typical House office has from twelve to seventeen people, with more than half working in one of the House office buildings. Space presents a problem, and offices are often overcrowded.

The personal staffs of senators are also divided into Washington and home state staffs. The Washington office would include the administrative assistant, who is the senator's surrogate, several legislative assistants, a press secretary, an office manager, a personal secretary, case workers, and other personnel. In addition, senators maintain several home state offices, employing field persons and caseworkers. The personal staffs of senators range from as few as twenty to as many as sixty employees. Nowadays, a senator from a large state can spend more than $1 million a year on salaries, while each of the 435 House members receives $288,156 for salaries. These salaries are justified by the lawmakers on the ground that they are forced to maintain large staffs to keep up with the rising demand for services from people back home—running down a pension check or helping someone get a small business loan. The functions of the personal staffs may be summarized as follows.

The administrative assistant (AA) is a jack-of-all-trades. A maxim of Capitol Hill is that if one cannot see the senator or congressman, the next best thing is to see the administrative assistant. He or she performs a number of functions. Visiting with constituents as a substitute for the legislator is a major chore of the administrative assistant. Another major responsibility is meeting with lobbyists and special interest groups. It is important to note that the more successful lobbyists understand this role and proceed accordingly. AAs are also often involved in handling constituency problems, such as casework and projects. An increasing number of people are utilizing their elected representatives to serve as an "appeals board" for adverse social security, veterans', OSHA, and other bureaucratic decisions. Supporting constituent project applications for such things as roads, dams, urban revitalization, and economic development are also a part of day-to-day activities. The AA is often a substitute for the boss at receptions, campaign activities, and other meetings. He or she usually runs the office staff, sometimes with the support of an executive assistant or office manager. Finally, answering opinion mail consumes a part of the AAs time.

The legislative assistant (LA) provides legislative and journalistic support to a member of Congress. The LA attends committee meetings and attempts to ensure that the member is kept informed of what is going on and that he or she is present at critical meetings. The role of the LA should not be overlooked when the member's committee attendance is desired. Often the LA will write House or Senate floor remarks and speeches for the member and will also perform legislative research, read, analyze, and draft bills. This legislative support role is a crucial factor in the development of legislation. On occasion, the LA will write articles, books, and speeches for the member to use outside Congress. For members who are anxious to make a national name for themselves, it pays to have bright LAs on their staffs to get them mentioned in magazine articles and newspaper headlines. Working with legislative correspondents, the LA also answers mail pertaining to legislative issues before the Congress.

The press secretary advertises the legislator through the

media—press, radio, and television. The previously cited statement by John L. Lewis, "He who doesn't toot his own horn, doesn't get it tooted," is applicable here. Most congressmen are smart enough to follow this rather fundamental axiom, particularly if they expect opposition in the general elections. It pays to brag to the home folks about the number of dams or urban renewal projects a congressman has supposedly delivered. The press secretary is usually a former member of the fourth estate, and thus can build on his or her contacts and friendships with the newspapers to sell the accomplishments of the boss. The role of the press secretary also includes managing radio and television appearances. He or she may also work on campaign issues and produce copy for magazine articles, books, and speeches. In some offices the administrative assistant may handle some legislative issues of relevance to the national press, while the press secretary is responsible for the district or state operations.

The personal secretary is the member's protector, scheduler, letter writer, and personal confidant. Sex stereotyping and male chauvinism aside, the personal secretary is often a single woman whose life is linked emotionally and occupationally to serving her boss. She is typically the most loyal staff member. When he moves up, say from the House to the Senate, she too will move up.[6] The personal secretary handles most personal letters, telegrams, and phone calls for the member. She is a key person to know when access to the member is desired—a most vital contact. But this generally holds true in private industry as well.

The receptionist is the first person to be seen when one enters a congressional office. She usually doubles as the office telephone switchboard operator, handling hundreds of calls each day. Greeting constituents and providing them with House and Senate gallery passes are among her duties. She also provides information about Washington attractions and handles the distribution of districts or state literature. She is of importance to a congressman in that initial impressions can create either a positive or negative image of office operations.

Office managers are utilized in larger offices on Capitol Hill. They make sure that the staff is properly supplied, that letters are answered, and that floor space is efficiently allocated. They supervise secretarial activities such as filing, mailing, and maintaining supply inventories. In a few congressional offices, executive assistants may perform many of these chores as well as provide support on legislative matters.

District or state offices usually include two or more caseworkers, a field person, and possibly an administrative assistant. Caseworkers handle veterans' problems, black-lung cases, social security claims, and other federal benefit programs. They may also assist constituents with state and local case problems. The field person travels around the district or state, meeting with constituents to discuss case problems, grants, and political matters. There was a time when one district office was sufficient for the great majority of congressmen; however, it is typical today to have about three offices. This reflects the increasing dependence of many groups in society on government largesse. Probably more important is the fact that several offices give the legislator greater visibility in the home district or state.

Functions of Committee and Subcommittee Staffs

There are committees and subcommittees galore in Congress, and each has its own staff. At last count there were more than 200 subcommittees, twice as many as in 1960. The largest have million-dollar budgets and thirty or more employees. The committees and subcommittees do everything imaginable. Some are important and others are much less important, but once created they rarely go out of business. The House Select Committee on the Outer Continental Shelf still has a $290,000 annual budget and twelve employees despite having completed its mission in 1978. As mentioned previously, the main struggle over legislation takes place in committees and especially in subcommittees, for this is where the basic work of Congress is done. A former Speaker of the House of Representatives has called committees "the eye, the ear, the hand, and very often the brain of the House." [7] They are separate centers of power, with rules, patterns of action, and internal processes of their own. Committees and subcommittees represent an attempt to have a broad division of labor in Congress. Within particular policy fields, there is a variety of areas of specialized competence that must be applied before the total picture can be understood. The committee system divides the legislative sphere into numerous specialized units.

Committee and subcommittee chairman can exercise considerable power over both the operations of their own units and the final output of Congress. There are also ranking minority party counterparts on each committee and subcommittee. They, too, have an important role in the committee process. The committee or subcommittee chairman and the ranking minority member are important contacts. But as is true in the operation of a congressional office, where the administrative assistant often runs the show while the congressman is out politicking, staff members can be the real power in a committee or subcommittee. The typical committee chairman also serves on other committees and has political responsibilities as well. The committee staff director, or majority counsel, can exert considerable influence upon the chairman with respect to legislative matters. The same holds true to a lesser degree for the minority member on the committee. If the chairman and the minority counterpart get along well, so much the better in terms of a quid pro quo relationship.

Committee and subcommittee staffs are divided into two categories: permanent and investigative. Permanent staff members are paid from funds allocated by previously enacted appropriations bills and are generally assigned to the chairman and ranking minority member of a committee or subcommittee. Investigative staff members are usually employed on a temporary basis, and their salaries are paid from funds appropriated each year by House and Senate resolutions. They are often assigned to subcommittee chairmen and their ranking minority counterparts. Each committee has a staff director, minority counsel, and chief clerk as well as professional staff. The Joint Economic Committee, for example, has a professional staff of fourteen economists, ten for the majority party and the remainder for the minority party. Subcommittees generally follow this same division of responsibility. Perhaps the most important thing to remember about committee and subcommittee staffs is that they work for a single person who is either the committee or subcommittee chairman or the ranking minority counterpart. They do not work for the committee or subcommittee.[8] Committee staff members are very much aware that one person, the chairman or the minority counterpart, hired them and can in turn fire them.

The staff director and minority counsel are engaged in working with other committees and supervising the clerical and professional staffs. They are the direct link between the staffs and the committee or subcommittee chairman and ranking minority member. They are responsible for overseeing budget considerations, drafting legislative plans, and ensuring that their bosses' interests are taken care of. They are responsible for holding hearings and arranging the order of witnesses. They are also responsible for the direction of staff studies. For businessmen who wish to provide input at a hearing or to the committee chairman, the staff director is the key contact. He or she is also a vital contact for lobbyists and pressure groups.

Committee professional staff members are actively involved in drafting bills and investigating issues of importance to the committee chairman. They are a source of information used to develop policy. In the course of their duties, they have almost daily contact with the bureaucracy in the executive branch of government and the independent agencies. Contact is usually made to discuss future legislation, implementation of a public law, information about a particular program or project, or any number of topics associated with program authorization, appropriation budgeting, or oversight. They also work with congressmen in holding hearings and in conferences and executive sessions. In some respects, their responsibilities are similar to those performed by personal staff aides—to meet with lobbyists, provide legislative expertise, and so forth. Unlike personal staff members, the majority of whom are from the home state or district of the member of Congress, professional staff members are usually from the immediate Washington area. Over three-quarters of professional staff members are male, causing equal rights advocates to contend that affirmative action should begin at home.

An overwhelming majority of professional staff members have had no business experience. They have usually moved into their jobs from various executive agencies or other Capitol Hill jobs. Very few have degrees in business administration or engineering; journalism, law, and political science are the most common areas of degree specialization. It is perhaps no wonder that these staff members often do not appreciate the concerns of business. However, not all of the blame can be attributed to the hiring practices of Congress. As a rule, business firms do not encourage their young professional employees to seek congressional internships, nor do they make government service a prerequisite for senior management positions.[9]

The statement is sometimes made on Capitol Hill that no two offices are organized the same way. This is not true. There are three basic types of personal and committee staff organizations: hierarchical, coordinative, and individualistic.[10] Hierarchical congressional offices or committees are run by an administrative assistant or a staff director, who reports directly to the congressman or committee chairman, with all the staff reporting to him. In coordinative congressional offices or committees, more than one person is responsible for reporting to the congressman or chairman. The administrative assistant, legislative assistant, and press secretary all report to the congressman, and each is responsible for defined staff functions. Individualistic office organizations have from three to a dozen staff members reporting to the congressman or committee chairman. The larger the congressional office or committee, the more likely it is to be organized along hierarchical lines. It is important to know how a staff is organized when following through the chain of command on issues that are being pursued. If the organization is hierarchical, the chain of command is less diffuse. It is directly from the administrative assistant to the congressman and the staff director to the committee chairman.

The Business Don'ts and Dos of Handling Staff Members

Personal, committee, and subcommittee staff members play a major role in running the legislative show—the invisible force in American lawmaking. In responding to currents of change in American society, Congress has become more and more specialized and is making increased use of professional experts for assistance in legislative decision-making. Assistants on committees, on the personal staffs of senators and representatives, and in central support groups such as the Library of Congress make up what some observers are calling the congressional bureaucracy. It is important for business to be aware of this bureaucracy because it does most of the work of Congress. There are rules for the care and feeding of this group:

Don't forget who they are. There are 20,000 staff members who answer letters and phone calls, draft legislation, think up ideas for legislation, set up hearings, draft amendments, and oversee implementation of public law. This work affects society as a whole. When business firms or the general public need congressional assistance, they are most likely to be the key figures involved.

Don't overestimate what they know. Many people have a tendency, when visiting a congressional office for the first time, to ascribe Olympian characteristics to its denizens. Like banks and funeral homes, there is a certain aura about a congressional office. However, this aura soon fades. Staff members need outside assistance. With more government programs than there are staff members in the entire Congress, no one member can have expertise but on a very few programs. They have to move frequently from subject area to subject area—health care to tariffs to tax policy, for example. They are knowledgeable about issues, but they are rarely experts on a given subject. They should be used as a conduit to reach a representative or a senator on a particular issue. This is sound business policy. Provide them with information that supports your case, and be frank and open about it.

Don't underestimate their power. As the currency of the congressional system, staff are the manifestation of power. Members of Congress trust them, support them, depend on them, and act on their suggestions. Be aware of these facts, and remember that they will most likely be next to the member at key decision points while you will not. Get to know key staff personally, and use your access through them to reach the member. This is a basic point. Be sure to respect the constraints placed on staff —lack of time, incomplete knowledge, member loyalty, and congressional office politics.

Don't trick them. A basic but not original maxim on Capitol Hill is "Don't get burned twice." A staffer given incomplete or inaccurate information will remember it until hell freezes over. Maintain your credibility by always stating your case accurately, completely, succinctly, and in a timely fashion.

Don't hesitate to ask for advice. Most staff members are flattered that you are interested in their opinions, since most people they see are only interested in giving opinions. You would be surprised at how intelligent they are. It is important to find out who is for and who is against a specific issue, or what needs to be done to gain support.

Do trust them. Most staffers can be trusted to try to do what they promise. But remember to follow up all requests and visits. Capitol Hill places inordinate demands on staffers; thus they may forget to act or act too late for your purposes. On Capitol Hill the future is two weeks away and the past is a week ago. If your request was made outside this time frame, then a follow-up is needed.

Do contact them on a regular basis. Each day a typical professional staff member receives on the average twenty-five phone calls, hundreds of pieces of mail, and visits by half a dozen people. One staff member created a contact file of 500 persons in her assigned legislative area within nine months. It is easy to forget a one-time contact, so it is necessary to keep one's name before the staff member.

Do visit before asking a favor. As mentioned previously, it is important to get to know legislators. It is also important to get to know their staffs before a favor can be requested. Human nature is such that friends and acquaintances are more likely to be listened to than a stranger with a cause who comes in off the street. It is perhaps easier to ask a congressman for a favor, particularly in an election year, than it is to ask a staff member. The latter sometimes requires more careful cultivation.

Do provide summarized, useful information. Congressional offices receive thousands of pieces of information each day by mail, telephone, telegrams, and personal visits. Information overload is a fact of life on Capitol Hill. Personal contact with a staff member is expedited by presenting a verbal summary of the relevant problem along with a concise written summation repeating the major points. Also let the staff member know that you can be called on to provide additional information if needed.

Do be frank and provide a pro and con analysis of issues when it is appropriate. A candid and open discussion with most staff members will redound to your advantage. A staff member can defend your case better if a true picture is presented. Few things can undermine the position of a business advocate more quickly than for a staff member to find out that he or she has not been given a complete description of the issue in question. Pro and con analysis is commonly used on Capitol Hill when staff members make presentations to committee chairmen. This technique is a quick and easy way to make your point where it counts the most—with those members of Congress who make the ultimate decisions. A staff member can always use input in an analysis of an issue.

Finally, hire the best staff members. They are receiving one of the most expensive educations known to man, in dealing with the most important decision-making apparatus in the United States—Congress. Staffers, along with their bosses, deal with billion-dollar decisions almost daily. After surviving three or four years in Congress, a staffer generally has become quite knowledgeable about many issues, the operation of committees and subcommittees, the Capitol Hill subculture, public and private interest groups, and the modus operandi of the federal government as a whole. Contacts are important on Capitol Hill, and special interest groups are recognizing this fact by hiring staff members.[11]

Congressional bureaucracy is unique. No other legislative body—national, state, or local—has the quality or quantity of staff assistance found within the U.S. Congress. With 535 separate congressional offices, more than 200 committee and subcommittee groups, legislative secretariats for each House, and support organizations, Congress qualifies as a complex organization. Thus congressional staffs, both committee and personal, have become an increasingly vital resource to members of Congress. As legislative decision making has become more complex and time-consuming, staffs have been expanded and the distribution of staff has been changed. New staff support groups have been created, and congressmen have come to view staff assistance as important to policy formation, constituent service, and the power acquisition that is central to congressional activity. It pays to know staff members, for they have access to the power structure and the capacity to significantly influence the decision-making process. It is not for nothing that they have been called "the invisible force in American lawmaking," the power behind the legislative throne.

10

Administrative Agencies

EVERY TYPE OF BUSINESS ENTERPRISE in the United States falls within at least the indirect influence of a number of government administrative agencies. These agencies carry out the administrative tasks of government and are usually called boards, commissions, or agencies. Administrative agencies acquire their authority to act from the legislative branch of government, and the legislation creating them is called an enabling act. They do most of the day-to-day work of government and, as a consequence, they make many significant policy decisions. Any business firm that fails to recognize this will not operate effectively and will lose an opportunity to influence changes that might benefit it. It is important to note that most enabling acts creating administrative agencies provide them with appreciable discretion to act on enforcing legislation. Thus, very broad and general standards may be constitutional, and few persons, including businessmen, have successfully challenged the actions of either federal or state agencies on the grounds that the act creating an agency did not include sufficient standards.

Administrative agencies perform two separate functions: They issue rules and regulations and they adjudicate cases. The

128

power to make rules and regulations is delegated to an agency by legislation; thus it is acting in the same manner as a legislature. For example, if an agency designates certain areas for smokers and nonsmokers, this action has the same legal effect as if it had been taken by Congress or a state legislature. The action becomes the law of the land. The judicial responsibilities of administrative agencies are quite important. They find facts and apply rules and regulations just as any court would. In carrying out the process of adjudication, federal and state agencies generally employ procedures similar to those used by the courts. The Administrative Procedure Act requires almost all federal agencies to meet certain standards in their procedures, so there is a similarity in enforcement by federal agencies in general.[1] State agencies frequently follow a similar pattern. In adjudication procedures, most agencies follow an investigation-complaint-hearing order. However, because of limited resources, agencies make an effort to prevent disputes from reaching the hearing stage, with the result that more than 90 percent of investigations of violations do not result in a hearing.

Work of Administrative Agencies

Since agencies have been created to deal with specific problems as they arise, the system of administrative agencies as a whole has not developed along planned lines. As a result of this lack of overall planning, the agencies differ greatly in their manner of operation and structure, and there are many instances of overlapping power and jurisdiction. During the past eighty years, whenever a problem requiring regulation became apparent, legislatures often reacted by creating an agency to do the job. Good examples can be found in the economic holocaust of the 1930s. A large number of administrative agencies were created to help solve the social, economic, and political problems that stemmed from the stock market crash of 1929 and the world depression that followed. Some of these, such as the Securities and Exchange Commission (SEC) and the National Labor Relations Board (NLRB), are still operative; others, such as the Reconstruction Finance Corporation, have ceased to exist. Many state and local agencies have also been created in response to the need for control. Today, when the traditional machinery of social control appears to be working inefficiently, the tendency is to seek to solve the problem by use of creation of an administrative agency.

Broad Powers

The power of those agencies that have the greatest impact on the business community is broad. These agencies, which include the Equal Employment Opportunity Commission (EOCC), Environmental Protection Agency (EPA), Occupational Safety and Health Administration (OSHA), Consumer Product Safety Commission (CPSC), Federal Trade Commission (FTC), Securities and Exchange Commission (SEC), and several others of the alphabet soup variety, generally have the power to make rules that have the force of law. An agency with this power is said to have quasi-legislative power. Many agencies also function as courts do. They settle disputes and they hear and decide upon violations of statutes or of their own rules. These activities are described as quasi-judicial. Finally, much of the work of agencies is administrative in nature. This covers a wide variety of duties, which include investigating firms in a given industry, determining if formal action should be initiated, and negotiating settlements. However, a substantial number of agencies have administrative responsibilities but do not have quasi-judicial or quasi-legislative power. What business firms have to face in their operations is a rather impressive array of government administrative agencies that regulate one or more facets of business decision-making.

Sanctions

Government intervention in business involves the threat and application of sanctions in order to achieve desired economic and social outcomes. When industry survival and/or industrial externalities such as pollution are of concern, sanctions may often be positive, taking the form of subsidies, tariffs, and tax incentives. When the target is the undesirable behavior of firms or groups of firms within an industry, negative sanctions are often used to induce compliance. These negative sanctions can designate noncompliance a criminal offense requiring the imposition of fines and/or imprisonment, or a civil offense involving the deprivation of the right or privilege to engage in economic transaction through the loss of licenses, permits, and franchises. For example, the Clean Air Act of 1970, which is administered by the Environmental Protection Agency, subjects willful polluters to fines of up to $50,000 a day and jail sentences of up to two years. Plants can be shut down and permits to operate canceled if pollution continues. Citizens and interest groups have the right to sue in federal court to force polluters, including the U.S. government, to cease and desist pollution practices.

In applying negative sanctions, the intent is to use the coercive powers of the state in order to obtain compliance. The purpose is to announce to society or to its components, including business, that various actions are not to be done and to insure that fewer of them are done. Business firms have no alternative but to comply with a mandatory standard if the regulatory agency has sufficient enforcement tools. In addition, the expected behavior of the regulatory agencies includes the actions of fact-finding, the application of the law to the facts, and the imposition of the appropriate sanctions where noncompliance has been found. Thus, the intent and process of regulation is more like adjudication than other types of political action. It can be said that violators of economic regulation differ from violators of criminal law only in terms of the degree of responsibility for societal harm that is attributed to these violators by policymakers, regulators, and the community as a whole. Firm owners and managers are generally held responsible only for their actions, which are often technical and morally neutral.

Independent Commissions

Administrative agencies can be divided into two categories: the independent regulatory commissions and those agencies that are a part of the executive branch of government. In many areas of domestic policy formulation, independent agencies exercise more important control; however, different economic and political needs have produced administrative agencies exercising vast legislative and adjudicative powers that do not fit the classification of independent regulatory agencies. Many executive agencies perform regulatory functions as part of a broader responsibility. Administrative functions, divided into legislative, judicial, and executive categories, are performed by all types of agencies; however, at the same time, agencies may differ with respect to the reasons for their creation, their principal goals, and their organizational structures. These factors are largely determined by the political forces that led to the creation of particular agencies and provide a basis for continuing support.

Federal Regulatory Agencies

Congress has assigned much responsibility for the execution of the laws to independent bodies known as regulatory agencies. With few exceptions, they are known as commissions. It is somewhat difficult to define what a regulatory agency is, however, and this difficulty of classification stems from the fact that Congress has not pursued a rational line in differentiating the independent agencies from those located in some executive departments. The regulation of stock exchanges, for example, has been delegated to the Securities and Exchange Commission, an independent agency, whereas, until recently, the regulation of commodity exchanges was under the jurisdiction of the executive branch of government. Similarly, misrepresentation of articles, including drugs, is the concern of an independent agency, whereas misleading labeling of food, drugs, and insecticides is the concern of an executive department.

In theory, these commissions have been established by Congress in order to regulate and control the economy in accordance with the will of Congress. The existence of such agencies is justified on the ground that the complexities of modern society demand regulation in order to avoid economic anarchy, monopoly, and irresponsibility. It has been argued, for example, that the advent of phenomena such as atomic energy and jet aircraft calls for greater surveillance by government in order to make appropriate use of these resources to promote the goals of modern society. From another perspective, the need for many regulatory agencies, such as the Interstate Commerce Commission, is often challenged on the ground that such regulation hinders free enterprise and encourages waste. These agencies also attract criticism because they are somewhat incompatible with the system of separation of powers. Their very existence represents a diffusion of executive power, which the Constitution vests in the president. This separate existence, however, is justified because these bodies perform not only executive functions, but legislative and judicial ones as well.

Their legislative functions principally concern the promulgation of regulations. Within a broad general policy laid down by Congress, the regulatory agencies issue rules and regulations from time to time. Proposals are first published in the *Federal Register,* and the affected parties are invited to respond to the proposal. Hearings and studies are made, usually within a sixty-day period, and a final determination is then made, subject to the approval of the president. Clearly, then, the agencies make law, just as Congress makes law, and the rules and regulations they establish can often be changed or reversed only by an act of Congress. Their judicial power may be seen in their power to enforce laws laid down by Congress and their own regulations through the adjudicatory process. In carrying out the will of Congress to discourage monopolistic enterprises, for example, the Federal Trade Commission has broad powers that affect such activities as mergers between competing corporations. In many instances, conflicts between the regulatory agencies and the private sector are resolved in actual cases before administrative tribunals.

The term *independent* suggests that the president has only limited control over these agencies and no direct responsibility for their decisions or actions. A few such agencies are located in the executive department, but most are not. In nearly every independent agency, the governing body is plural in character, headed by a chairman. To encourage their independence from both the president and a single political party, Congress has established overlapping terms of office so that no one president can pack an agency with his or her followers. This attempt to keep the agencies above politics is further strengthened by limitations laid down by Congress as to the number of commissioners who may be appointed from any one political party. In addition, the length of the terms tends to make even a president's own appointees somewhat independent; however, in spite of this and of their structural independence from the executive branch, the major regulatory agencies are in reality subject to appreciable executive influence. A member of the presidential staff may attempt to persuade a commissioner to adopt the president's position. Executive influence may also be asserted through the budgetary process. Agency requests for funds go through the Bureau of the Budget and as a result are subject to executive surveillance.

To a lesser extent, these regulatory agencies are also subject to Congress and the courts. Congress establishes their jurisdiction and defines their powers but has limited control over their budgets and their personnel, nor can members of Congress interfere with the day-to-day operations of these agencies or attempt to intervene in agency proceedings. Agencies that have been created by Congress can also be terminated by legislative action; however, the threat of termination is not taken very seriously. Most legislative influence on agencies is the result of the agencies' dependence on Congress for financial support. For example, during the early 1920s, adverse congressional reaction to the Federal Trade Commission's investigation of the meat-packing industry led to a reduction in the funds available to that agency. Personnel had to be discharged, Congress transferred jurisdiction over meat packing to the Department of Agriculture, and, in addition, the agency was denied appropriations for other investigations that it had planned. As a result of legislative domination of funds needed by the agencies, agency personnel sometimes tend to be oversolicitous of the opinions of individual legislators who are in a position to block bills that will fund the agency's operations.

Courts do not play a direct role in the adjudication of cases that are brought before the agencies. Cases decided by the agencies may, however, be appealed to the federal courts, giving the latter the power of judicial review of agency rulings.

When an agency has acted in an adjudicative context, the courts can review its procedures to ensure that they are constitutionally valid, that the agency had proper jurisdiction, and that the statutory rules controlling procedures have been observed. They may also review the agency's interpretation of the law, but the courts exercise substantial restraint in this area, and their powers are limited. Nevertheless, judicial review of agency actions is a valuable right for the business community to have. Review by the courts of agency decisions provides a safeguard against administrative excesses and the unfair or arbitrary action of overzealous officials. The circumstances in which a court exercising judicial review will be most likely to set aside an agency ruling are those in which an agency has erred in its interpretation of a statute, has acted outside the scope of its authority, or appears to have denied due process because of unfair agency procedures.

Independent State Commissions

States, too, have independent commissions to regulate intrastate activities. In fact, the states were the first to become involved in the commission form of regulation. Public utility regulation in the United States first developed at the state level. In the 1870s the agricultural states of the Middle West began to limit freight rates and to curtail railroad rate discrimination in response to political pressures exercised by the Grange. The right of a state to regulate public utilities was tested in the 1877 landmark *Munn* v. *Illinois* case, when the U.S. Supreme Court declared constitutional an Illinois law that regulated the rates and practices of grain elevators.[2] State public utility laws and public utility commissions developed rapidly thereafter. It became evident that the rapidity of economic change required constant, day-to-day regulation and legislatures were only in session for a few months of the year, many for only a few weeks. Courts, too, were not equipped to regulate commerce. What was needed were regulatory agencies that could devote full-time attention to the control of a specific area of activity and could employ persons with expertise on the subject of regulation.

In the individual states, authority to regulate is derived from the police power of the state, the authority of a sovereign state to legislate for the protection of the health, safety, morals, and general welfare of its citizens. The courts have given the states extremely wide latitude under these powers to regulate all kinds of business activities. In *Nebbia* v. *New York,* a 1934 case, the Supreme Court decided "a state is free to adopt whatever economic policy may reasonably be deemed to promote the public welfare and to enforce that policy by legislation adapted to its purpose." [3] Thus the right of federal and state governments to regulate economic activity—particularly to set prices or rates—is clearly established, although the courts recognize that such regulation cannot violate individual rights safeguarded by the Constitution and that the activities of all regulatory bodies must be subject to judicial review. When the police power of the states comes into conflict with the federal government, the states must yield.

The constitution and laws of each state define more or less specifically the powers and duties of commissions under their jurisdiction; consequently, there is great variation in the laws of the states and in the responsibilities of their commissions. In most states, public utility commissions have power to regulate the rates charged by privately owned utilities, but the scope of jurisdiction is not the same for all states. In a few, the control is limited to the fixing of maximum rates only, leaving the companies free to set rates lower than the maximum fixed by the commission. In most states, the commission have the power to regulate the rates paid to privately owned utilities by municipalities for street lighting, lighting of public buildings, and other public services. They also may regulate the rates paid to a privately owned utility by the federal government. The authority of state commissions to regulate contracts between municipal utilities and ultimate consumers is the same that is applicable to private utilities in those states where the commissions have jurisdiction over the municipal utilities. The power to regulate special contracts between utilities is granted under the commission's authority to regulate rates.

Members of state regulatory commissions are either appointed by the governor with the approval of the legislature or are elected by direct popular vote. There are defects in both approaches. Appointments are often based on factors that have nothing to do with the qualifications necessary to become a competent public service commissioner. Favoritism and politics are often involved in appointments. To some extent, overlapping terms for state commissioners prevent purely political appointees beholden to special interests. Elected officials are presumed to be more responsive to the public will, but that is not necessarily the case. A commissioner who is a good campaigner may not possess the requisite skills to understand the complex nature of the work of commissions. In many states, salaries are inadequate to attract and hold the type of person needed on the commissions. Because of the complicated and technical character of the duties of a state commissioner, it requires three or four years for the typical appointee or elected official to acquire the experience and information necessary to handle the responsibilities of the office properly.

Administrative Agencies in Executive Departments

It would be a mistake to think that the only regulatory agencies are the independent commissions. The system of administrative agencies as a whole has not developed along planned lines, since the process leading to their creation is highly political, and administrative functions and organization are essentially determined by political factors. There is not necessarily any logic to organizational standards in American bureaucracy, or at least not enough logic for general agreement that a given form of organization should be used when certain functions are to be performed. As a result of a lack of overall planning, agencies differ greatly in manner of operation and structure, and there are many instances of overlapping power and jurisdiction. However, some regulatory fields are relatively narrow and are more easily and conveniently put under the jurisdiction of a department that possesses responsibility for a broad but related field. For example, the Commodity Credit Corporation is part of the Department of Agriculture.

Most regulatory agencies that function with executive departments possess both quasi-legislative and quasi-judicial powers just like the independent regulatory commissions. The power to make rules and regulations has been delegated to these agencies by legislative fiat. The only important difference between an agency rule and a law enacted by a legislative body is that the rule may be slightly more susceptible to attack because it was not made by elected officials. Administrative agencies can also implement policy or legislation through a process of initiating and settling specific cases. They engage in administrative adjudication, which encompasses procedures used in deciding cases. In many types of cases the procedures are carefully outlined. Hearings are frequently prescribed, records are required to be kept, and so on. Further, there are often elaborate provisions for judicial review, which suggests that if the agencies step beyond the boundaries of legitimate authority, redress can always be secured in the courts. However, the scope of judicial review of particular administrative agency decisions is limited, the logic being that the agency, rather than the court, is supposed to be the expert in the field in which it has been empowered to act. Clearly, a court can reverse any action taken by an agency that is outside the scope of the agency's jurisdiction.

The Courts and Administrative Agencies

In spite of its limitations, judicial review of administrative agency actions is a valuable right and safeguard for the business community. Alexander Hamilton once stated that judicial independence is necessary "to guard the Constitution and the rights of individuals from the effects of those ill humors, which the arts of designing men, or the influence of particular conjunctures, sometimes disseminate among themselves, and which, though they speedily give place to better information, and more deliberate reflection, have a tendency, in the meantime, to occasion dangerous innovations in the government and in the minor party in the community." [4] What this rather turgid statement means is that review by the courts of agency decisions provides a protection against administrative excesses. Judicial independence is important to protect the rights of individuals and groups and to shape the way in which laws are implemented. Judges are supposed to protect the people from themselves, a job they could not perform properly if they were dependent upon the people directly, or indirectly by being responsible to the legislature.

There has, however, been a transfer of some judicial power to the administrative agencies. In the past, the courts have exercised not only all judicial functions, but what in modern technology would be called administrative functions. For example, during the colonial period and most of the nineteenth century the courts acted as rate-making bodies, setting tolls charged for public roads and rates charged by railroads. They possessed various kinds of regulatory powers, and in terms of the common law, they were the correct repositories of such power.[5] In many instances the courts developed general rules through case-by-case determinations that became, in effect, legislation. In the absence of interest by legislative bodies, it was only natural that the courts should step in to establish such rules. The courts thus resembled modern administrative agencies, possessing almost unchecked legislative and judicial power. Before statutory standards were created, there were all sorts of common-law rules governing how an employee could receive compensation for an injury resulting from his employment. The common law was substantive as well as procedural in nature, and in both respects it was shaped entirely by judicial action.

At present, antitrust litigation provides a good example of a field in which primary jurisdiction resides in the courts. The Justice Department must rely entirely on the judiciary for enforcement. Many other agencies engaged in antitrust enforcement have varying degrees of power independent of the courts, most notably the Federal Trade Commission, but even it shares powers with the judiciary to some extent. The Justice Department acts as the primary prosecuting body. It cannot act independently to prevent restraints of trade because Congress has been unwilling to give it this power ever since it passed the Sherman Act in 1890. Once again it is important to note that the extent of judicial power over administrative agencies is determined by Congress, except as constitutional issues may be involved; in that case the courts will take jurisdiction regardless of congressional intent to the contrary.

Those who have the power to implement the law through judicial interpretation have, in effect, the power to control exactly what criteria will be used. Because the common-law courts in the past were unable to change the substantive criteria of the law, the only way legislative bodies could assure the implementation of new and different standards was to create new agencies for enforcement; hence the administrative agency has become a common device to circumvent the courts and the substantive standards they insisted upon. Administrative agencies, as agents of Congress, reflect group demands for positive action. They are not supposed to be arbiters like the courts. They are active and initiate policy in accordance with their policy interests. For example, when the FTC ferrets out deceptive practices, either through its own investigations or through information gained from an outside source, it initiates action in the name of the FTC against the party involved. It then adjudicates the very case it initiates. If the case reaches a formal hearing and goes to a hearing examiner for an initial decision, it is not at that point subject to commission control. However, after the examiner renders the decision, the commission may reverse it. The result is that the FTC can control the decisions rendered in most of the cases it initiates.

In subsequent chapters, some of the more important regulatory agencies will be discussed. These agencies can be divided into two categories, old line and new line. The term *old line* refers to the fact that certain independent commissions were created to regulate a specific industry, for example, the Civil Aeronautics Board (CAB) to regulate airlines and the Interstate Commerce Commission (ICC) to regulate railroads. The goals of these commissions were economic in nature. The Civil Aeronautics Act of 1938 created the CAB and gave it regulatory authority over entry, rates, airmail payments, and subsidies of common carriers. The new line commissions, such as the CPSC, cut across virtually every branch of private industry. Environmental controls apply to most companies, as do requirements concerning job safety and occupational health and safety standards. The goals of the new line commissions are much more social in nature. The CPSC, for example, possesses the authority to set mandatory safety standards for consumer products and to ban or recall these products from the marketplace.

It is important to know how to deal with the various regulatory agencies. The business advocacy relationship must also be applied to those agencies that have an impact upon the decision-making process. Effective cooperation between business and the administrative agencies has been hampered by differences in philosophical attitudes that are more negative than positive. An antipathy has always existed between the two institutions that has inhibited close working relationships and continues today. Many persons view closer working relationships between government and business with alarm or skepticism, feeling that business will dominate government or government will dominate business. However, American society now confronts socioeconomic problems of great complexity, the resolutions of which require much closer cooperation between business and government.

11

The Major Regulatory Agencies

VERY FEW BUSINESS FIRMS are free from having to deal with regulatory agencies. The extent of their regulation is of concern to business leaders and to many economists. If just the basic federal government regulations were compiled into a book, a shelf of over fifteen feet would be needed to hold the more than 60,000 pages of fine print.[1] Federal agencies send out over 10,000 different forms a year, and business spends an estimated $20 billion completing them. The total annual cost to the consumer of all regulatory activities is put at over $100 billion a year.[2]

There are those who feel that government has passed the optimum point of intervention in business and that unresponsive bureaucracy and cumbersome rules of enforcement are stifling business initiative. The power of bureaucrats and their involvement in the politics of national policy is a dominant fact of life in contemporary American society. Conflicts over rules or standards do not stop with the passage of laws; decisions have to be made as to how the laws are going to be applied. Hence many political decisions are merely transferred or delegated from those who make the laws to the bureaucrats who enforce them.

It is important to become familiar with those regulatory agencies that have the greatest impact upon business. The functions of these agencies are varied, reflecting, in part, the time period in which they were created. For example, the Federal Trade Commission (FTC) was created during the early part of this century when the primary concern of government was to promote competition in the marketplace and to protect business and consumers against anticompetitive business practices. Other agencies were created during the Depression as a reaction against certain business abuses that developed during the 1920s. The Securities and Exchange Commission (SEC) is a case in point. Then there are those agencies that regulate natural monopolies such as electric power companies; an example would be the Federal Power Commission (FPC). Finally, there are the regulatory agencies with social goals, such as the Equal Employment Opportunity Commission (EOCC). The rationale for these agencies is that the market system does not work to solve the problem of externalities or side effects. Take pollution as an example. There was no price imposed on business for using the air and water to store or discharge its waste. Therefore, the cost to society of polluting the air was not taken into account by market forces. The government stepped in to impose regulations and to create the Environmental Protection Agency (EPA).

The Federal Trade Commission (FTC)

Few regulatory agencies have more impact upon business than the FTC. It was created by the Federal Trade Commission Act of 1914 with the intent of preventing unfair business methods of competition. It was given the power to prevent persons or corporations, except banks and common carriers subject to the various acts that regulate interstate commerce, from using unfair methods of competition in commerce. It was also given the power to investigate the practices of business combinations and to conduct hearings. It was authorized to issue cease-and-desist orders and to apply to a circuit court of appeals to enforce them. A violation is punishable by contempt of court. In addition to cease-and-desist orders, the commission was given the power to negotiate terms of agreement, known as consent decrees, violations of which are cause for court action. The commission was also given joint responsibility with the Justice Department for enforcing certain prohibitions of the Clayton Act, in particular those prohibitions that deal with various forms of price discrimination.[3]

The FTC has come to be an all-purpose agency. Not only does it administer the antitrust laws of the United States, but a wide variety of other laws as well. The Wheeler-Lea Act of 1938 authorizes the FTC to protect the public by preventing the dissemination of false or misleading advertisements with respect to food and drugs. Various labeling acts are also under the jurisdiction of the FTC. The Wool Products Labeling Act and the Fur Products Labeling Act are examples. The McCarran Insurance Act of 1948 gives the commission partial jurisdiction over the insurance industry. This activity is complex because it varies from state to state with variations in state law. Then there is the Consumer Credit Protection Act of 1968, or, as it is more commonly called, the Truth-in-Lending Act, which requires that borrowers be made aware of basic information about the cost and terms of credit. Finally, there is the Consumer Product Warranty Act of 1975, which provides minimum disclosure standards for written consumer product warranties and defines federal content standards for these warranties. The act also extended the consumer protection powers of the FTC to cover local consumer abuses when state or local protection programs are inadequate.

The FTC is currently one of the most controversial regulatory agencies in Washington. It has been accused many times of either insufficient regulation or regulation too oriented to the needs of a given industry and not to the needs of the public. It has also been accused of too much regulation, with the result that the individual, the economy, in fact society as a whole, is stifled. This condemnation is given added weight because critics are able to point to specific instances where the FTC has not performed well. Congress has recently voiced its criticism of the FTC, taking the position that it has overstepped its authority. It accuses the FTC of excessive paternalism and of being overzealous in its enforcement efforts. The attempt of the FTC to regulate "kid vid," the content and advertising on cartoons and children's programs, has drawn criticism. Congress has threatened to curb the authority of the FTC unless it tones down the intensity of some of its activities. This reflects the current antiregulatory sentiments of Congress.

The Consumer Product Safety Commission (CPSC)

The Consumer Product Safety Act of 1972 created the five-member CPSC, which functions as an independent regulatory agency. The commission is regarded by some as the most powerful regulatory agency in Washington.[4] It has jurisdiction over more than 10,000 consumer products and has the power to inspect facilities where consumer goods are manufactured, stored, or transported. The commission can also require all manufacturers, private labelers, and distributors to establish and maintain books and records and to make available additional information as it deems necessary. It can require the use of specific labels that set forth the results of product testing. This requirement has its most important impact in the production process, where the design of numerous products must conform to federal standards. Since safety standards are formulated at various governmental and independent testing stations, a manufacturer may find that a finished product no longer meets federal standards, and product lines may have to be altered drastically.

Section 15 of the Consumer Product Safety Act requires a company to take corrective steps if it becomes aware of the fact that a product either fails to comply with an applicable safety rule or contains a defect that could create a substantial product hazard. The company has to inform the CPSC of the defect. If, after investigation, the commission determines that a product hazard exists, the company, or a distributor or retailer for that matter, may be required to publicize the information to consumers. The commission can compel a manufacturer to refund the purchase price of the product, less a reasonable allowance for use, or to replace the product with a like or equivalent product that complies with the consumer product safety rule. The cost of product recalls can be considerable. It cost General Motors $3.5 million for postage alone to notify by certified mail, as required by law, the 6.5 million owners of cars with questionable engine mounts.[5] Moreover, liability is assumed for injuries to the consumer when the results of such injury are reasonably forseeable, regardless of whether the product is itself dangerous or harmful. A consumer need not prove that a manufacturer was guilty of negligence.

The Environmental Protection Agency (EPA)

In July 1970, President Nixon submitted to Congress a reorganization plan to create an independent environmental protection agency. The organization was approved, and the EPA was created. Functions that had been vested in the Department of the Interior relating to studies on the effects of insecticides and pesticides in the United States were transferred to this agency. Also transferred were functions vested in the Department of Health, Education, and Welfare, including the creation of tolerance norms for pesticide chemicals under the Food, Drug, and Cosmetics Act. The EPA was given supervision over air pollution standards as set in the Clean Air Act of 1970 and its subsequent amendments. The EPA was also given jurisdiction over water pollution control programs, particularly those set forth in the Water Pollution Control Act of 1972, including the setting of water quality standards. The jurisdiction of the EPA was extended further to apply to the Noise Control Act of 1972, and it became responsible for setting noise emission standards for products that have been identified as major sources of noise. The EPA now has jurisdiction over the major federal environmental laws passed during the last decade.

The impact of the EPA upon business is considerable. In addition to the paperwork requirements, which are particularly onerous to small firms, and the delays in regulation, there is the cost of compliance with the requirements of the various acts the EPA administers. In terms of real resource costs, one estimate projected a real cost of $81.4 billion invested in capital equipment and $121.8 billion spent on operation and maintenance to comply with the Clean Air Act and the Water Pollution Act over a ten-year period from 1973 to 1982.[6] There is also a substantial reallocation of real resources to the purpose of cleaning up the environment. In 1976, for example, the estimated real resource allocation devoted to cleaning up the environment amounted to 1.7 percent of the real gross national product.[7] Since that time, the real resource allocation devoted to pollution control has increased to 2.2 percent of real gross national product.

The cost of pollution control can also be expressed on an industry and firm basis. Rightly or wrongly, the steel industry blames its problems in a competitive world market on the cost of compliance with environmental laws. The industry has spent $4 billion on environmental controls and expects to have to pay out another $4 billion over the next three to five years.[8] As a result, the steel companies contend their operations are barely profitable. Chrysler argues that its financial problems are to a major degree caused by the cost of compliance with environmental laws; it costs Chrysler roughly twice as much per car compared with General Motors to comply with environmental requirements. A study of government regulatory costs prepared by Arthur Anderson and Company indicated that for forty-eight companies in the study, EPA regulations accounted for by far the heaviest regulatory burden in comparison with five other federal regulatory agencies.[9] In fact, EPA regulations accounted for $2 billion in incremental costs for the forty-eight companies, or 77 percent of the combined incremental costs of the agencies used in the study.[10] These costs did not reflect other incremental costs imposed by environmental requirements of the Bureau of Land Management.

The Equal Employment Opportunity Commission (EEOC)

The EEOC was created by the Civil Rights Act of 1964. Its enforcement authority was greatly increased by the Equal Employment Opportunity Act of 1972. The EEOC has the authority to investigate and act on a charge of a pattern or practice of discrimination, whether filed by or on behalf of a person or group claiming to be aggrieved or by a member of the commission. The EEOC has the right to initiate civil suits against employees, labor unions, and any group accused of practicing employment discrimination. In this connection, it might be added that private individuals and groups have the right to sue under Title VII of the Civil Rights Act of 1964. The EEOC also has the right to investigate company records to see if a pattern of discrimination exists and to subpoena company records if necessary. Every employer, labor union, and organization subject to the Civil Rights Act and subsequent executive orders must keep records relevant to the determination of whether unlawful practices have been committed and must furnish to the EEOC a detailed description of the manner in which persons are selected to participate in job training programs.

Legal remedies under the Civil Rights Act and related executive orders of the president range from cease-and-desist orders through individual reinstatement and group preferential hiring to the cutting off of all federal contracts with the offending employer. Lawsuits may also be filed under the provisions of the Equal Employment Opportunity Act of 1972. The most important leverage the federal government possesses to enforce compliance with affirmative action goals is the money it spends. One way or another, most business firms derive some part of their revenue from federal government spending. The loss of a contract means a loss of revenue. This is a virtual sentence of death to a research firm or a university, for they are dependent upon federal money to maintain their competitive standing. Moreover, there is always the possibility of lawsuits of the type that led to American Telephone and Telegraph's (AT&T) $75 million settlement upon employees who had charged that discrimination had deprived them of past promotions and raises.[11] This settlement involved the principle of restitution, which can be quite costly if applied to a business firm. AT&T had to pay restitution to its women and minority employees as compensation for promotions and raises they did not receive because of their sex or color.[12]

There are several incremental costs involved in complying

with EEOC regulations. First, there is the paperwork factor. The volume of resources required to process data, formulate policies, make reports, and conduct communications with a variety of federal officials is a large, direct, and unavoidable cost to any employer, whether or not the employer is guilty of anything, and whether or not any legal sanction is ever imposed.[13] Hiring has been changed by outside pressures, so that it now generates much more paperwork as evidence of "good faith" hiring efforts, and in general hiring has become slower, more laborious, more costly, and less certain. It is not that it costs more to hire women and minorities, but that it becomes more costly to hire anyone. Second, there is the incremental cost of affirmative action training programs for women and minorities. This cost can be considerable. In the previously mentioned Arthur Anderson and Company study of regulatory costs of forty-eight firms, 76 percent of the incremental costs incurred in compliance with equal employment opportunity regulations were attributable to affirmative action programs for women and minorities.

The Occupational Safety and Health Administration (OSHA)

The OSHA was created as a Department of Labor agency to administer the Occupational Safety and Health Act of 1970. The purpose of the act is "to assure safe and healthful working conditions for working men and women." [14] It requires employers to comply with safety and health standards promulgated by OSHA. In addition, every employer is required to furnish for each of his employees a job "free from recognized hazards that are causing or likely to cause death or serious physical harm." [15] While this "general duty" clause might appear to be an all-encompassing requirement for the provision of safety, it was clearly the intent of Congress that the clause be limited in scope and relied upon infrequently. "Recognized hazards" are defined in the congressional debate as those that can be detected by the common human senses, unaided by testing devices, and which are generally known in the industry as hazards.[16] Further, a firm can be penalized under the "general duty" clause only if the unsafe condition has been cited by an inspector and the employer has refused to correct it in the specified time.

"When I use a word," Humpty Dumpty said to Alice, "it means just what I choose it to mean." [17] OSHA is fond of words of its choosing as witnessed by the following example:

> The general slope of grain and that in areas of local deviations of grain must not be steeper than 1 in 15 in rungs and cleats. For all ladders cross grain not steeper than 1 in 12 are permitted in lieu of 1 in 15, provided the size is increased to afford at least 15 percent greater calculated strength for ladders built to minimum dimensions. Local deviations of grain associated with otherwise permissible irregularities are permitted.[18]

This gem is a part of the 140-odd regulations pertaining to portable wood ladders. The standards OSHA enforces cover 800 pages in the *Code of Federal Regulations* and number close to 4,400, with 2,100 applying to all industries and the remainder to construction and maritime industries.[19]

The reach and authority of OSHA is considerable. If inspection discloses a violation, the employer is cited, ordered to comply within a specific abatement period, and may be fined. Serious violations, ones that create a substantial probability of death or serious physical harm, must be fined up to $1,000 for each violation, but fines for each nonserious violation, although permitted, are not required. Willful or repeated violations may result in a civil penalty of $10,000 for each violation, and failure to correct a violation within a prescribed period may result in a fine of $1,000 per day. The only criminal penalties for violations of standards are imposed on willful violations that lead to the death of an employee; in these cases, a fine up to $10,000 and a jail sentence of up to six months are authorized.[20] Employers may appeal cited violations to OSHA, a three-member body appointed by the president.

OSHA has been the bane of many an employer's existence. Its rules often have been capricious and have conflicted with the rules of other regulatory agencies. A president of a small company complains, "The United States Department of Agriculture requires that our kitchen floors be washed repeatedly for sanitary purposes, yet OSHA rules that floors must be dry. What is a man to do?" [21] His statement reflects a problem of many employers, namely, the need for help in interpreting conflicting standards promulgated by various federal regulatory agencies. Part of OSHA's problem apparently is being unable to distinguish between serious health hazards and mere trivia. However, efforts have been made to make OSHA more efficient. The number of rules and regulations has been reduced, and some employers have been exempted from OSHA jurisdiction. Also, many of the costs required by original OSHA regulations have already been absorbed. Workers have been provided with such things as goggles and other safety devices, and factories have installed fire suppression equipment and other safety systems.

Other Regulatory Agencies

The regulatory agencies just discussed probably have the most impact upon the majority of business firms. They by no means exhaust the total number of federal regulatory agencies that have an effect upon business. There is the SEC, created by the Securities Exchange Act of 1934, which is responsible for the regulation of securities and financial markets and of electric and gas public utility holding companies. With the Justice Department, the SEC is also responsible for administering the Foreign Corrupt Practices Act. The accounting provisions of this act represent an extension of the SEC's power from requiring companies whose securities are publicly traded to file accurate reports with the SEC, to requiring these companies to keep accurate records. The accounting provisions apply whether or not bribery is involved. The unclear language of the act's anti-bribery provisions is estimated to cost U.S. businesses $1 billion a year in lost trade.[22]

The Food and Drug Administration (FDA), part of the Department of Health and Human Resources, was created by the Pure Food and Drug Act of 1906, which is considered to be the first significant piece of consumer protection legislation in U.S.

history. The Food, Drug, and Cosmetics Act of 1938 gave the FDA authority to inspect factories producing food, drugs, and cosmetics and empowered it to license manufacturers and establish standards for granting licenses when the processing of foodstuffs might involve a risk of contamination that would be a menace to public health. In 1962 this act was amended to extend the mandate and regulatory control of the FDA in several ways. First, firms were required to provide documented scientific evidence regarding a new drug's efficacy in addition to the proof of safety required by the 1938 act. Second, the amendments gave the FDA, for the first time, discretionary power over the clinical research process. For example, before any tests on humans can be conducted, firms are now required to submit a new drug investigational plan, giving the results of animal tests and proposing the research protocols for human tests. Third, the amendments imposed regulatory controls on the advertising and promotion of prescription drugs. In particular, firms must restrict advertising claims to those approved by the FDA in labeling and packaging inserts.[23]

Then there are those federal regulatory commissions that have jurisdiction over the interstate activities of the natural monopolies and the transportation industry. These are the Interstate Commerce Commission, the Federal Communications Commission, and the Federal Power Commission.[24] Their efforts are concentrated on regulating a specific industry—railroads, television, oil pipelines, for example. Their powers are broad, and they have the authority to make rules that have the force of law. Each commission possesses a somewhat different rationale and mode of regulation. For example, regulation of radio and television includes licensing and limited control over service quality but essentially no control over pricing. Regulation of electric and gas companies, on the other hand, involves considerable control over pricing. Although these commissions are set up to regulate specific industries, they have some impact upon all industries. Costs and regulatory inefficiencies imposed by the Interstate Commerce Commission on railroads are felt by business firms that depend on the railroads for transportation.

Regulatory requirements are also imposed by the Department of Energy (DOE), in particular in such areas as fuel usage and pricing, energy conservation programs, and administrative costs. Price controls on natural gas have been cited by the oil and gas industries as one of the reasons curtailments have been necessary. The low price of natural gas relative to other fuels has encouraged its use and discouraged conservation. Controls have limited the incentives to find and produce more natural gas, contributing to an imbalance betweeen supply and demand. There has also been a conflict between the objectives of the DOE and the EPA in the natural gas area. In 1977, the DOE was pushing for the use of coal rather than natural gas, while the EPA was attempting to control coal stack emissions. Coal does not burn as cleanly as natural gas, and its use has intensified the concern about ambient air quality.

Issues of Regulation

During the 1970s, the pace of government regulation of the U.S. economy increased, particularly in the areas of health, safety, and environmental protection. Many of these regulations, however, impose a substantial compliance cost—as much as $100 billion per year, according to one study.[25] Much of this cost is considered necessary and beneficial to society as a whole, such as the protection of workers from factory accidents and consumers from defective products. Much of this cost is also unnecessary, the result of excessive and duplicative regulations that produce little more than higher business costs and higher prices. Difficulties have arisen because government has attempted to solve various problems by the use of control devices, including threats. A former chairman of the CPSC once said, "If a company violates our statute, we will not concern ourselves with its middle-level executives; we will put the chief executive in jail. Once we do put a top executive behind bars, I am sure that we will get a much higher degree of cooperation." [26] This statement did little to foster better business-government relations.

There are, of course, alternatives. Reflecting the current mood in Congress toward less government regulation, liberals have joined conservatives in believing that instead of trying to write detailed rules and regulations, the federal government should impose certain general obligations on business and provide a reasonably easy way for penalties to be imposed. An example would be to make it costly for businesses not to adopt safety standards, but to allow the details of administration to be worked out by the thousands of businesses rather than by some government agency. This approach would tend to dilute some of the problems and criticisms of regulation—the disruption of the operation of the market, disincentives to invest, costs of regulatory delays, and misallocation of resources. For example, delays caused by regulation in constructing the trans-Alaska pipeline and in bringing offshore oil wells into production have had a deleterious effect on jobs, supplies of petroleum, and the balance of payments.

Some economists argue for a regulatory budget.[27] They make the point that social regulation is the only institution without a budget constraint. In most institutions that are a part of American society, the use of resources is constrained, at least to some degree, by a budget. Households, firms, most government agencies, and the military services are operated with budgetary limitations. Only the regulatory agencies are not subject to limits imposed by a budget; thus there is no mechanism that forces agency decision makers to trade off expenditures on one goal for outlays on another. In the absence of a regulatory budget, regulators may proceed as if the resources they command have no other social value. Resources used in one way could be devoted to other uses. For example, resources devoted to environmental protection could also be used to enhance the quality of life by increasing the supply of food, shelter, and clothing. There is a need for a mechanism to ensure that society has enough environmental protection and that in the process it does not lose too much of other social outputs.

Society would gain from the use of a regulatory budget in two ways. First, the imposition of a regulatory budget would require congressional action on the size of the federal budget. This would focus attention on the benefits of regulation. How would the EPA, for example, be given the right to command, say, $30 or $40 billion per year without some evidence that it is providing the public with commensurate value in the form of a cleaner, safer environment? Without some attempt to measure benefits, it would be difficult to argue for $30 billion rather than perhaps $25 billion. Secondly, a regulatory budget would require each regulator to make trade-offs across various policies. Pursuing very tight standards for ozone, which is not very harmful to humans at low concentrations, would reduce EPA's "budget" allocation for toxic substances and carcinogens, which are more harmful. Very soon, each agency's management would begin demanding staff estimates of alternative standards and of the cost of different degrees of regulatory stringency because each decision would affect the value of regulatory options available elsewhere. Cost-benefit analysis would become an important tool for regulators, not just a concept to be avoided if possible.

12

Dealing with Regulatory Agencies

"CONTRARIWISE," said Tweedledum to Alice, "if it was so, it might be; and if it were so, it would be; but as it isn't, it ain't. That's logic." [1] Many business firms feel that government regulatory agencies possess the same convoluted type of logic. The number, variety, and extent of government programs to regulate business have revealed numerous deficiencies in the very process of regulation. The ubiquitous hamburger, staple of the fast-food trade, is the subject of 41,000 federal and state regulations, many of them stemming from 200 laws and 111,000 precedent-setting court cases. It is estimated that these regulations add 8 to 11 cents a pound to the cost of hamburger. The steel industry alone has to comply with some 5,600 regulations administered by 26 federal agencies. [2]

Perhaps even worse than overregulation is the fact the government regulators often have a compulsion to fix things that are not broken. The Consumer Product Safety Commission (CPSC), for example, ordered formal hearings to determine if four million electric frying pans were hazardous. The interesting point is that out of the four million frying pans, not a single injury had been reported to the commission.

Very few business firms are free from having to deal with regulatory agencies. Thus, it is in the interest of business to provide some input into decisions that will ultimately affect their operation. Because participation in the regulatory process is expensive, the effectiveness with which a business can protect its interests depends upon the resources it has available. Not all firms will have equal input in the decision-making process. As a natural consequence of the adversary relationship between government and business, information flowing to regulatory agencies can be systematically biased against unrepresented business groups. Therefore, it is necessary to develop lines of communication between business firms and regulatory agencies. While direct confrontation and litigation may still be the norm, in certain quarters new methods, such as mediation, negotiation, dispute resolution, and conflict avoidance, are being tried. William K. Reilly, president of the Conservation Foundation, notes that a new era of environmental politics involving mediation is gaining popularity. He states that this method of problem solving "is less fraught with confrontation and adversary stalemates and recourse to the courts—approaches that have characterized much of our environmental protection action." [3]

It is desirable to examine the ways in which three very diverse companies handled their problems with regulatory agencies. Their strategies ranged from the adversary, or "head butting" approach, to the advocacy, or "sugar is better than vinegar" approach. The Marlin Toy Company case is perhaps the most important in that it illustrates the extent of federal regulatory power over business and how lack of prudence and care in the exercise of this power can mean financial disaster for a company unable to deal effectively with the regulatory bureaucracy. It also illustrates the point that small business firms are far from immune to government regulation; to the contrary, it is estimated that as many as 140,000 small business firms are fined each year for violating rules too complex or technical for their owners to understand.[4] Although the case may be atypical, it does illustrate that government is not omniscient, and that big government can create as many problems as big business or big labor. Moreover, there is little redress for the errors of big government.

Consumer Protection: The Marlin Toy Case

During the 1970s, public concern over the quality and safety of consumer products placed increasing demands upon the federal government to intercede on behalf of consumers in the sale of goods and services. Two major consumer acts were passed: the Consumer Product Safety Act of 1972, which created the CPSC, and the Consumer Product Warranty Act of 1975, which, among other things, strengthened the authority of the Federal Trade Commission (FTC) in the area of consumer protection. Proposals were also made to create a super government agency called the Consumer Protection Agency, but efforts failed in Congress.[5] In some states, agencies of this nature were created. At all levels of government there was an upsurge of consumer regulatory activity that directly affected American business. However, consumer protection laws do not come without costs. In addition to the cost of paperwork and the cost of compliance with government-mandated standards, there are other costs to business firms, consumers, and society as a whole. There is, for example, the cost to a business firm that can result from an incompetent ruling by a regulatory agency. The Marlin Toy Company is a case in point.

The Marlin Toy Company of Horicon, Wisconsin, provided jobs for 85 of the town's 1,400 residents.[6] The two most important products of this company, accounting for about 40 percent of its business, were two toys known as the Birdie Ball and the Flutter Ball. One was a transparent plastic sphere containing artificial birds and tiny, bright-colored plastic pellets, and the other was a similar sphere containing pellets and artificial butterflies. In November 1972 the Food and Drug Administration (FDA) notified the Marlin Toy Company that both toys were unsafe, reasoning that if a sphere broke, a child might be tempted to eat the pellets. However, since Marlin had first marketed the toys in 1962, not one person had complained to the company of any harm coming from them. The toys had already passed three safety tests—Marlin's, an insurance company's, and a department store's. Nevertheless, Marlin agreed to recall the spheres and remove the pellets. Within a month, the FDA said it was satisfied and promised to remove the toys from the next published list of banned products. But the list of banned products is released only once every six months, and Marlin lost a considerable part of its Christmas 1972 toy sales, in addition to its loss through recall of the banned toys.[7]

In anticipation of 1973 Christmas sales, the Marlin Toy Company began to increase production toward the end of the year. In September 1973, the newly formed CPSC published a special holiday list of dangerous toys whose sale was prohibited; this list included the toys Marlin had redesigned months before to the satisfaction of the FDA. Most unfortunately for Marlin, a typographical error had been made, and the new list should not have contained the company's products. By the time this error was acknowledged, it was too late. Stores all over the country had canceled their toy orders from the company for the 1973 Christmas season. By January 1974 the company was faced with bankruptcy, having lost at least $1.7 million in sales, which does not include what had been lost in goodwill.[8]

In March 1974, Ed Sohmers, general manager of the Marlin Toy Company, decided to take legal action against the CPSC. He turned to a New York City law firm for assistance and was quickly notified by a sympathetic lawyer that federal laws do not permit legal action against a federal agency in those instances where the agency has neglectfully misrepresented a product. Marlin's only recourse to justice, the lawyer advised, was a private bill in the Congress for relief. Turning to Wisconsin's senators and congressmen for support, the Marlin Toy Company was able to persuade them to introduce a private bill in the summer of 1974, with the support of the CPSC, which admitted its error. Unfortunately for the company, it takes a minimum of two years before any relief bill can be passed. Very few private relief bills are cleared by Congress, and those granting financial aid must be processed through the U.S. Court of Claims. This was hardly reassuring to the Marlin Toy Company.

Like most businesses subjected to government regulation, the Marlin Toy Company obeyed the law and put its trust in the hands of the federal bureaucracy. The company did not have full knowledge of the procedures of the CPSC, nor was it aware of the delays and confusion that often exist in large federal agencies. Because it did not seek corrective action until it was too late, the company suffered severe, if not irreparable, damage that could have been avoided. Marlin should have taken the following steps:

1. When first notified in November 1972 that its toys were on the FDA's proscribed list, Marlin should have challenged the FDA's ruling, employing the services of a Washington law firm to examine the government agency's testing procedures.
2. The company should have contacted the two Wisconsin senators, Nelson and Proxmire, and the congressman representing the district in which it is located.
3. After the FDA agreed to remove the banned toys from the list, the company should have sought verification when the revised list was released six months later.
4. When the CPSC issued an incorrect list of banned toys, the company should have contacted the Washington law firm and the Wisconsin senators asking them to intervene.

The Marlin Toy Company case does not have a happy ending, for the company had to get out of the toy business. The financial damage that resulted from the error made by the CPSC was irreparable.[9] Although the money bill introduced by the two Wisconsin senators was approved by Congress, the money appropriated for compensation was only a fraction of the losses sustained as a result of the error: a reported $40,000 compared with losses of millions of dollars. To date the owner has not received even this token compensation. It should be added that this compensation will not even cover the legal fees incurred in handling the case. The equipment of the toy company, including the toy molds, was sold to other toy companies. The Marlin Electric Company, a companion company, which made fuse mounts, survived and was sold by the owner to outside interests. The company is now in the business of making fuse mounts, circuit breakers, and other electric components. In discussing the result of the case, the former owner was understandably disgusted by the whole affair: the loss of revenue through no fault of the company, the legal fees incurred in the settlement, and the nonpayment of the settlement, which doesn't cover the legal fees, much less the business losses incurred as a result of the error.

How Not to Respond to a Regulatory Agency: The Firestone Company

A successful corporation must not only sell products, but it must also be perceived as having integrity and a willingness to serve the public interest. The radial tire controversy in which Firestone is involved is a classic example of how not to take on a federal agency. As *Fortune* magazine said,

> What seems clear is that Firestone, in its attempts to ward off disagreeable consequences and defend its honor, has been its own worst enemy. At times, it has almost gone out of its way to provoke suspicion and doubt. One would expect a company convinced of its rectitude to cooperate fully with the government. But Firestone has repeatedly tried to thwart investigations of its radial tire, and has publicly impugned the motives of the investigators as well. In the process, it has simply prolonged and intensified its ordeal.[10]

The result of Firestone's intransigence is that it has lost money, sales, and image; the last it is trying to recover by hiring the respected actor James Stewart to extol the craftmanship philosophy of the company's founder, Harvey Firestone.

Firestone's troubles began in 1976, when the Center for Auto Safety received an inordinate number of complaints about the company's 500 radial tire. The director of the center wrote to the president of Firestone and the National Highway Traffic Safety Administration (NHTSA) noting the complaints. The NHTSA recommended that the radial tire be recalled. Firestone responded by accusing Ralph Nader's former associates Joan Claybrook, chairwoman of the NHTSA, Clarence Ditlow, director of the Center for Highway Safety, and Clarence Dodge, special counsel for a House investigative committee, of getting together to play Ping-Pong or badminton with Firestone.[11] The company also tried to restrain the release of a Traffic Safety Administration survey of radial tire owners that gave the Firestone 500 radial tire a poor rating. Despite a court order not to disseminate its findings, the survey was eventually released and was widely reported in the press. Firestone's image was damaged when the study was made public, and it finally consented to a partial recall of the tires. Subsequent events have continued to overwhelm Firestone. Over 250 law suits have been filed, and settlements have ranged up to $1.5 million.

Those who are responsible for the management of Firestone have made it the most visible defier of government regulation. While this may be popular in some circles, it does not make good business sense. The net result has been a drastic drop in sales and profits, and more important, a drop in confidence in Firestone products. The company engaged in an adversary relationship with the government regulators, a no-win proposition, as it found out. A more appropriate approach for Firestone would have been to:

1. Allow all facts, opinions, and conjectures to be aired.
2. Build a case for its radial tires based on its own research and surveys of Firestone tire owners.
3. Work with the regulatory agencies in an attempt to negotiate an outcome, perhaps unsatisfactory to it and the agencies, but at least acceptable to public opinion.
4. Be prepared at public appearances before congressional committees, regulatory agencies, and the press. Emphasis should have been placed on company attempts to overcome the problem of the radial tire, rather than posing conspiracy theories to denigrate the regulatory agencies.
5. Be candid with all those who were involved in the radial tire controversy, and exercise strong and visible corporate leadership, particularly at the highest echelons of management. This should have been done through public appearances and announcements.

Firestone, as well as many other firms fighting regulatory battles, lost the battle within the political marketplace because it did not choose to fight by the new rules. Just as Pickett's charge at Gettysburg came to naught against the entrenched

Yankee artillery and sharpshooters, Firestone's charge was doomed before it had begun. But this is not to exculpate the regulatory agencies, for regulation does cost money. The degree of regulation of business life in the United States is quite awesome in its range and scope. Probably not one area of business activity today is untouched by some kind of government regulation. The central question is not the efficacy of any particular agency or specific issue of regulation, but the regulatory process itself and its consequences for the corporation and for American society.

How Best to Work within the Regulatory Framework: The Dow Chemical Company

The Dow Chemical Company is probably not any more enthusiastic about government regulation than any other American company. However, it accepts regulation as a fact of life, realizing that it is necessary, while overregulation is wasteful and expensive. Dow feels that little has been done to put into operation promised cuts in excess regulation. A Dow-financed regulatory impact study determined that federal regulation cost the company $147 million and $186 million in 1975 and 1976. Of this two-year total of $333 million, $119 million was attributed to what Dow called excessive and unnecessary regulation.[12] One purpose of this study was to examine and evaluate the impact of federal regulatory activity and to develop regulatory cost data upon which to base realistic guidelines that could prove useful to government. Another purpose of the study was to share methodology and results with other companies so that they might better assess their own regulatory costs. Dow's work in determining regulatory impact and pursuing positive regulatory change merits duplication by other corporations, close attention by government regulatory decision makers, and wide public distribution. This strategy is positive, for it facilitates an advocacy rather than an adversary approach. It provides a detailed data base that allows an analysis of regulatory impact and whether it is excessive and needs to be modified. Government regulatory agencies will find that impact studies can provide useful information as a basis to review regulatory decisions.

The main hope for a less abrasive business-government relationship lies in the emergence of a better integrated and more mature society. Regulatory enforcement is essentially a political process entailing bargaining between partners of unequal power. Sometimes the greater power is in the hands of the regulatory agency, sometimes in the hands of business. But the faulty interaction between business and government needs correction. Business no longer can occupy an essentially separate part of the social spectrum with concerns and interests divergent from, it not antagonistic to, those of government. There are certain considerations that must be resolved. For example, what constitutes the optimum combination of market arrangements and government intervention? What policies provide the best framework within which the market mechanism can operate?

Dealing with Government Executives and Their Bureaucracies

Many of the rules that apply to business dealings with legislatures and regulatory agencies also apply to dealing with executives at all levels of government and the bureaucracies they administer. The executive role, however, is transitory, for most executives are appointed by the president, a governor, or a mayor, as opposed to the more permanent and career-oriented bureaucracy. Government executives and their staffs serve as conduits to the bureaucracy. The bureaucrat is supposed to be familiar with a given problem and can be reached, if necessary, through an executive or his or her staff. The bureaucrat can also be reached through a legislator. In fact, when serious problems arise, it is often advisable to seek assistance from bureaucrats by using executives and legislators as intermediaries.

Corporate dealings with executives and the bureaucracies they administer can be divided into a political approach and a product approach. The former involves seeking assistance with specific business problems; the latter is concerned with contracts and project proposals. The political approach typically involves the attainment of information about a specific problem, such as taxes, pensions, or plant safety procedures. It is difficult to know whom to contact, for there is a myriad of government agencies. If the problem concerns a tax ruling, it is often desirable to call or write the executive under whose jurisdiction the tax agency falls. The inquiry will be forwarded to the agency for response either to the business or to the executive. In some cases, it is feasible to ask a legislator to act as an intermediary. This approach is often the quickest, for no agency can afford to ignore a legislative request.

Government is the single largest purchasing unit in the United States, and most business firms derive at least a part of their sales from government spending. Business firms provide such things as dams, sewage systems, airports, roads, military material, and educational facilities. The government process of awarding contracts can be time consuming, and often it is necessary to expedite action. This can be done in the following manner. The Washington representative of a major construction company, for example, calls the home district congressman and complains that a contract has been pending with the Department of Transportation (DOT) for a year. A staff member agrees to look into the matter and requests the contract number. Then contact is made with the congressional liaison officer at the DOT. Usually the contact is made on a first name basis, for many contacts have already been made. The appropriate information will be obtained and then imparted to the Washington representative, who in turn will inform the company. Then the company knows where it stands. Contacts are quite important in doing business with government, for they can circumvent any unnecessary spinning of wheels.

Executives often have the final say over what their bureaucracies can do. The power of these bureaucrats and their involvement in the politics of national policy is a dominant fact of life in contemporary American politics. Career administrators in particular have influence. They have more bargaining and alliance-building skills than the elected and appointed officials to whom they report. Career administrators develop a keen sensitivity to the political pressures playing on their agencies or bureaus. They are heavily involved with members of Congress, for they have control over agency budgets and the power to approve or deny requests for needed legislation. An agency is especially careful to develop good relations with members of committees and subcommittees handling its legislation and appropriations. It would be foolish not to do so. Special interest groups make it a point to nurture close ties with both Congress and agency and bureau heads. By the same token, Congress and the agencies and bureaus cultivate each other and thus various alliances are built up. A quid pro quo relationship exists; however, Congress is the senior partner in the alliance, as the following example illustrates:

> SUBCOMMITTEE CHAIRMAN: I wrote you gentlemen a polite letter about it, and no action was taken. Now Savannah may be unimportant to the Weather Bureau, but it is important to me.
>
> WEATHER BUREAU OFFICIAL: I can almost commit ourselves to seeing to it that the Savannah weather report gets distribution in the northeastern United States [source of tourists for the subcommittee chairman's district].[13]

Like Congress, the bureaucracy must obtain political support before embarking upon new legislative programs, but in many instances it either possesses such support from clientele groups or has the tools to achieve it without much trouble. Administrative policies have virtually automatic political support, which in turn will have some impact upon Congress.[14] Politics—conflicts over who is to get what and who is to do what—do not stop. Of course the policy established by Congress counts; it alters subsequent political conflict in many ways. But decisions still need to be made as the policy is applied to specific situations. Hence many decisions are transferred from the legislators to the bureaucrats.

A Postscript

The current business-government relationship has been described by many business observers as adversary in nature. Officials of government look upon themselves as probers, inspectors, taxers, regulators, and punishers of business transgressions. Businessmen typically view government agencies as obstacles, constraints, delayers, and impediments to economic progress, having much power to stop and little to start. A considerable measure of suspicion prevails. The current relationship is seriously defective, and it must be improved if American society is to make satisfactory progress toward its goals. These goals have become more numerous, more complex, more interrelated, and more difficult to reconcile as society has become more affluent. Business has often been accused of being insensitive to changing social values and of being obstructive rather than facilitative in adjusting to them. Faced with a multiplicity of pressures and goals, business firms will run a considerable risk if they act independently. There must be increased and improved interaction between business and government in developing a consensus that will allow realization of individual freedom within the framework of the common welfare.

13

Lobbying: Is It a Dirty Word?

THE TITLE OF A RECENT ARTICLE in *Parade* magazine was "Lobbyists: The Unelected Lawmakers in Washington." [1] Jack Anderson, the well-known columnist and author of the article, makes the point that lobbyists affect our country's life from the cradle to the grave. He is not very complimentary toward lobbyists. Lobbyists traffic in favors and in return provide political donations and reelection campaign workers. Usually it is the accumulation of small gratuities rather than any direct bribe that gradually obligates the people in power. They become cozy with lobbyists, heed their advice, introduce their legislation, and make speeches written by them. So it is that special interest groups, represented by lobbyists, help write the legislation and shape the government rulings that affect everything from the price of gasoline to the care of the sick. Lobbying on Capitol Hill has become so flagrant that no member of Congress is safe from temptation. An estimated 15,000 lobbyists prowl the Capitol's corridors and lobby in behalf of their clients, who range from the American College of Obstetricians and Gynecologists to the Casket Manufacturers Association.

As long as we have a democratic system of government, there

will be people seeking favors. In the past, persons and groups seeking favors from elected officials provided monetary and/or material inducements to specific individuals in hopes of currying favor and special treatment. The Grant and Harding administrations are remembered primarily for their generosity to special interest groups: in the case of Grant, the railroads, and in the case of Harding, the oil companies. Harding's father is reported to have said, "Warren, it is a good thing you are not a woman, for you would be in a family way all the time. You can't say no to anyone." Thus, the well-known abuses of a few lobbyists and elected officials have provided reasons for the average citizen to recoil in horror when the word *lobbyist* is mentioned. A Nashville, Tennessee, television show, "The Nashville Advocate," asked viewers to mail in their answers to the question "Do lobbyists serve the public interest?" More than 87 percent of the respondents said no.[2] Perhaps this is a general indictment of the way in which our government works and of the groups that try to influence it.

As the United States has grown in size and population, so has the diversity of opinion. This has been especially true during the last twenty years, as many special interest groups have developed to demand a voice in the determination of resource allocation. The civil rights, antiwar, and consumer movements have reflected the growing desire of citizens to organize and state their positions effectively. Most legislative and executive policy decisions are implemented by persons acting under the influence of groups. As our country has become more institutionally complex, the ability of the federal government to reflect the interests of all citizens and groups of citizens has lessened. Our system has developed many access points—the courts, regulatory agencies, Congress and the Executive Office of the President—where individuals and groups can present their views. This diversity of access does take its toll on efficiency, but it helps to ensure input into the decision-making process. People with authority in government expect to be lobbied; if they are not, then they may not be able to evaluate all sides of a given subject.

Nevertheless, it is important to be aware of the public's view of lobbying to keep strategic planning in perspective. It is no joking matter that lobbying is crucial to the operation of government, but it is also viewed by most citizens as inimical to the public interest. Blame for this attitude can be attributed to some extent to lobbyists, to civics and government teachers, and to all of us as individuals—until we become more aware of how government works. The vitality of a group or an individual rests, in part, on its acceptance by those around it. Most people are reacting to the publicized abuses of lobbyists when they say that lobbying is bad. If "The Nashville Advocate" had phrased its question a little differently to say, "Should an individual or group be heard by our government?" a different response might have been elicited. Most elected officials expect to hear about their constituencies' interests, and lobbying is one way these interests can be expressed.

Forms of Lobbying

Not too many years ago, lobbying, for the most part, meant a person representing a major group or organization before the legislature. Now it can take many forms: The Department of Defense may lobby the National Rifle Association or vice versa, the governor of Florida may lobby the Department of Transportation, and the Federal Trade Commission may lobby Congress. The mayor of Seattle could lobby the Executive Office of the president. All branches of government are subject to lobbying, even the courts. In general, however, there are three basic forms of lobbying in Washington: public and private lobbying of the various branches of government, but particularly the legislative branch; intergovernmental lobbying and intragovernmental lobbying.

Public and Private Organization Lobbying

The main focus, as far as this book is concerned, is on lobbying by public and private organizations. These groups lobby at all three policy-making stages: program/idea formulation; legislative development; and program implementation, regulation, and administration. Program/idea formulation involves selling an idea. Thousands of ideas float around Washington every day; for example, "Wouldn't it be great if we had a simple tax system?" or "We could do away with unemployment if we gave business firms the right incentives." Most ideas remain exactly that, for they are never systematically investigated or made a part of an organization's policy objectives. A first step in dealing with new ideas is to identify goals and objectives. Where do we want to end up? What issues do we currently face or could we be expected to face in the future?

After the issues have been identified, a priority-setting exercise should follow. Using means-and-ends statements, issues should be classified as being those of crucial and immediate importance, those of secondary importance, and those that are worthy of keeping an eye on. The last category may include hundreds of potential issues. The first and most important category must of necessity be kept short. Just as a congressman or the president tends to lose effectiveness when he tries to push more than five or six major policy initiatives, so should a business be wary of overextending its resources, credibility, and influence. Careful selection of major policy issues in the business-government milieu is mandatory. This selection should be subjected to some method of accountability.

Once a decision has been made to push an idea, it is desirable to put together a "package deal" that contains an enumeration of public and private needs and impacts, including the effect on employment, gross national product, tax revenues, and productivity, as well as a list of background materials—books, magazines, and resource documents. Pro and con analysis can also be used in selling government policymakers an idea. Public and private needs can be derived from public and private opinion polls, marketing surveys, public statements by individuals and organizations, futuristic projections, general analytical treatises, and academic treatment of political, economic, social, and religious issues. This is the key component of the "package deal," for concurrence on the importance of an idea helps to ensure its consideration in the political marketplace. A receptive audience can reduce the chances of outright rejection of an idea and can induce more careful consideration. The "package deal" can be used to lobby Congress, regulatory agencies, the courts, and the Executive Office of the President. This is where an idea is turned into policy—legislation, executive order, or regulation. Chances of acceptance can be improved by convincing policymakers of the viability of the idea.[3]

The process of how a bill becomes law has already been diagramed and discussed in Chapter 7. However, all branches of government contribute to the legislative process. To focus attention on Congress is only half the battle, for other branches of government also support their favorite programs and can lobby Congress to their ends. There is, of course, a working relationship among Congress, the administrative agencies, and the Executive Office of the President, and all participate in the shaping of legislation, although Congress ultimately passes the laws. Lobbying, then, can become an all-inclusive proposition. A premium is paid to those lobbyists who are prepared, who are able to mobilize their resources quickly, who have both strategic and tactical game plans, and who know the Washington scene.

Willie Sutton, the well-known bank robber and con artist, was once asked, "Why do you rob banks?" His utilitarian reply was, "That's where the money is." A parallel question posed to a politician might be, "How do you keep your support?" and the answer would probably be, "Doing what the voters want." Congressmen listen to their constituents, particularly if they are organized, because they vote. One member of Congress, who is apparently a consummate pragmatist, puts the matter rather succinctly:

> All of us who have been around the process very long realize that politics is not a hobby—it's a business. The bottom line is not profit or loss, it's votes. A congressman's profit is more votes than a competitor can get. That puts him in the black. So whatever contributes to his getting a profit in the next election instead of a deficit, which is fatal, is the motivator for him. A lot of people sneer at this and say it creates only a weathervane, thoughtless robots, but that's the way our system is. The members of the Congress are supposed to reflect the will of the people of the United States. So they do that.[4]

A trade association recently sought the support of a Kentucky senator on an issue. Word went out to the membership that the senator was in a key position to decide on the issue that was important to the association but was leaning toward an opposing point of view. On the day the trade association was to testify before the senator's subcommittee, a member of the association was recognized by the senator. He had been a pallbearer at the senator's mother's funeral and was a lifelong resident of the senator's hometown. The senator was then much more willing to hear the point of view of the association and eventually reversed his position. This example illustrates the point that little things can count in terms of political influence.

A successful trade association lobbyist has found that a college or a university in the congressman's district may have an expert who can best represent the association's point of view. An example can be noted. A Maryland congressman had listened for many hours to testimony on an issue before his subcommittee. Many of the nation's leading experts from Harvard, Massachusetts Institute of Technology, and the Rand Corporation had testified. Near the end of the day an expert from a university in the congressman's district appeared to testify. The congressman became more interested and listened to the testimony of his constituent. Not only did the voter/expert get the attention of the congressman, but his fee was a good deal lower than those paid to the national experts. In both these examples, legislators were influenced by their own constituents.

There are other points to note in lobbying Congress. First of all, one company, unless it is very large, cannot lobby effectively by itself. It is important to coordinate efforts with other companies with similar aims. It is also important to support trade associations, the chamber of commerce, and other groups with similar interests. Second, contacts can become fluid. The "old boy" syndrome is a thing of the past. There was a time when knowing the right "old boys" was sufficient, but a new age is upon us. A "new boy" network is created at the beginning of each Congress and new administration, while the "old boys" become lobbyists or return to Peoria. It is important to keep contacts with the state congressional delegation, the Executive Office of the President, and various administrative agencies that have an impact upon company operations. Keep up contacts through regular communication, and continue to take inventory of valuable resource points—for example, do you know someone in a newly created agency or subcommittee? Finally, it is important to know when to fight and when to compromise. The facts of legislative battles are that nobody wins unconditionally. Persons who can compromise know what one side will give up and the other side will accept.

Lobbying before Other Branches of Government

The various administrative agencies and their bureaucracies have a different constituency from the president and Congress. Their bottom line is not votes, nor is it profit or loss. It is running government, and run it they will. They have an idea that government should be run in the public interest, but their notion of the public interest can be different from that of the public's. The decision-making power of the typical bureaucrat is limited by statute, executive order, and regulation. Often the legislative history of a bill is used to help the bureaucrat make a decision. However, many bureaucrats will listen to viewpoints presented by business, often with less bias than congressmen or congressional staffers. It is important, however, to present a complete analysis of the issues involved, including impact on employment and productivity, background materials, and so forth. The nuts-and-bolts decisions on how business will be affected by regulation are made by the bureaucrats. Make sure they are given the chance to make the right decisions.

Leverage is of importance in lobbying. It would be inefficient to consider lobbying a one-branch-of-government phenomenon. Use the leverage of Congress, the Executive Office of the President, trade associations, and the judiciary to support a point of view. Congressmen make scores of inquiries each day for business firms concerning the interpretation and implementation of rules and regulations. They will often assume a strong advocacy role in support of business. In some cases, Congress may introduce legislation to overturn an adverse regulatory decision. Even though some political science textbooks state that the president rules the executive departments, this is hardly the case. In a discussion with one of his top administrators, Franklin D. Roosevelt is reported to have said:

When I woke up this morning, the first thing I saw was a head-line in the *New York Times* to the effect that our Navy was going to spend two billion dollars on a shipbuilding program. Here am I, the Commander in Chief of the Navy, having to read about that for the first time in the press. Do you know what I said to that?

No, Mr. President.

I said, Jesus Chr-rist! [5]

Because of limited resources, the Executive Office of the President cannot follow through on most business cases with the bureaucracy. The most successful approach is to have a trade association or the U.S. Chamber of Commerce contact the Executive Office of the President and note the generic nature of the problem. Each president has a person responsible for the concerns of business. This person has a small staff. Another approach, which is often quite successful, is to contact political appointees through a friendly intermediary in the appropriate department or agency. As with Congress, previous contacts, be they political or otherwise, are a prime desideratum in gaining sympathetic treatment and positive action. The president stands at the center of a complex and diverse system of government, and he, like all politicians and agencies, must strive to maintain a balance of political support in his favor. But the president cannot simply order something to be done and expect it to happen. If an administrative agency wishes to challenge a presidential decision, it can do so provided it has the support of Congress and its clientele groups.

Supervision and control over the implementation of legislation is performed by the Executive Office of the President and Congress. Because both lack adequate staff to follow all legislative programs, there is heavy dependence on outside review. Business firms should be aware of the oversight methods of control. For example, during congressional confirmation of executive appointees, certain guarantees can be obtained for the review of problem areas. Congressional committees and subcommittees can be encouraged to hold oversight hearings regarding inequities and mismanagement in the implementation of a particular program. The legislative veto can be used directly or indirectly as a threat to future programs. Recisions and deferrals of budgeted funds by the president can terminate or delay implementation. These are but a few of the techniques that can be used for supervision and control.

Intergovernmental Lobbying

A review of the budgets of state and local governments clearly indicates that the federal government is vital to their operations. Nearly $100 billion passes annually from Washington to state and local governments in the form of grants and other types of financial assistance. Such issues as revenue sharing, welfare policies, unemployment insurance, highway aid, and child care are at the heart of the federal-state and federal-local relationships. These relationships are of extreme importance to Washington. States, cities, and counties all have representatives who actively lobby the federal government for assistance. Examples are the American Association of State Highway Officials, the Council of State Governments, the National Association of Counties, and the National League of Cities. Representatives of these and similar organizations are concerned about many of the same problems that face the business community. They are interested in influencing legislation and dealing with the federal government on terms favorable to their interests. State and local government lobbyists should not be overlooked by business when it comes to seeking support for certain issues.

Intragovernmental Lobbying

Not only do state and local governments lobby in Washington, but the federal government lobbies itself. Lobbying occurs between the Executive Office of the President and the bureaucracy, regulatory agencies and Congress, the Defense Department and Congress, the president and Congress, and so forth. The president has lobbied Congress since the first days of the republic. A formal network exists today that is composed of over 650 people and costs around $15 million annually.[6] Its purpose is to place the president's views before Congress. The foremost lobbying organization in the country is not the National Association of Manufacturing or the National Rifle Association or the AFL-CIO. It is the White House and the executive branch. Even though Title 18 of the U.S. Code places serious restrictions on executive lobbying,[7] the White House does not hesitate to orchestrate massive efforts to influence congressional decision-making. It is the most potent, influential, and active lobbyist in Washington, according to former Senate Majority Leader Robert C. Byrd of West Virginia.[8] The president justifies his lobbying on the grounds that Article II of the Constitution allows him to provide Congress with information on the state of the union and to recommend to Congress measures necessary for the public welfare.

Each of the last four presidents has used slightly different congressional lobbying strategies. Lyndon Johnson placed all congressional liaison activities under White House control. Congressional relations staff from the executive departments would meet at the White House to receive specific assignments for work that needed to be done that week. These assignments regularly carried the department-level people outside their own legislative bailiwicks.[9] Personal knowledge of a member of Congress and his district were considered more important than substantive expertise in lobbying. The Johnson style of intra-governmental lobbying was centralized with an emphasis on the personal touch. But Johnson himself was a master at lobbying when he was Senate majority leader. He was effective when it came to getting things done. His personal touch with Congress carried over into the White House, where his effectiveness in getting legislation passed can be contrasted quite sharply with Jimmy Carter's.

Presidential lobbying was a little different during the Nixon administration. Bill Timmons, a well-known Washington lobbyist,[10] headed a seven-man congressional liaison operation. He was assisted by Tom Korologus, who headed Senate liaison efforts, and Max Friedersdorf, who was responsible for maintaining a liaison with the House. An average day started early for these men and their subordinates. At 7:30 A.M. they met with Office of Management and Budget (OMB) and Domestic Council aides to get a fix on the day's problems and to establish policy positions. The OMB and Domestic Council reviewed legislative positions on Capitol Hill. The staff would meet with Bill

Timmons at 8:00, then Timmons would meet with Nixon's senior advisers—Kissinger, Haig, and others—to review the
problems of the day.[11] The Nixon White House utilized its
congressional relations staff as a conduit to Capitol Hill in a
decentralized manner. It can be added that Gerald Ford's approach to congressional liaison work was the same, with the
same emphasis placed upon lobbying expertise and knowledge
of the subject.[12]

The Carter administration, at least during the first two years,
set some sort of record for poor lobbying activities. Carter himself had campaigned as not being a part of the "Washington
crowd," which was fine until he got to Washington. His relations with Congress were very poor, and lobbying efforts were
abysmal in terms of results. There was no coordination between
the White House and Congress. By 1978, however, liaison activities had improved. A manifestation of this was the House
vote on the B-1 bomber. Thirty-one House members were per-
suaded to change their votes to support the president's attempt
to kill construction of the B-1. Frank B. Moore, chief of
congressional relations in the Carter White House, met regularly with senior congressional relations people from various
departments and agencies. Each person produced a written
report of a few pages. Important legislative developments, both
present and upcoming, were discussed.[13] The reports were dis-
tilled by Moore's staff to roughly ten pages of weekend reading
for President Carter when Congress was in session.

The Ins and Outs of Lobbying

A basic truism in Washington is that there is someone who
knows everything about the thing you want to know; moreover,
he or she is just a few phone calls away. Finding the right
person to lobby for a point of view is easy. Many persons assume that lobbying activities begin with a congressman or cabinet member, such as the secretary of commerce. It is not
necessary to start this high; contacting senior bureaucrats and
congressional staff members is often the best way to begin.
They can often give advice on how to proceed and tactics to use

to gain support. Bureaucrats operate within subject areas of expertise, while congressmen operate within general legislative areas. Heads of regulatory commissions operate within specifically defined jurisdictional areas. If the objective is to sell a legislative idea in the tax area, contact a congressman on the House Ways and Means Committee or on the Senate Finance Committee. If the concern is with the survival of a certain animal, contact an endangered species expert at the Department of the Interior. If the issue is children's television advertising, contact a representative of the Federal Trade Commission.

Choosing the meeting place can make a difference in lobbying effectiveness. To meet a member of a consumer-oriented regulatory commission at one of Washington's fancy restaurants, such as Sans Souci, will probably not get a business lobbyist very far. It is more appropriate to meet at the commission during normal working hours. A congressman is best approached in the district or state. In Washington, there are constant interruptions—roll call votes, constituent visits, staff inquiries, and political activities. Getting attention and holding it for even a few minutes is difficult. There are fewer interruptions in the home base, and the congressman has more time to listen to constituent problems. So careful thought must be given in selecting the choice of a place in which to lobby effectively. Also, be prompt once a place and time have been set.

Timing is of prime importance in lobbying. The best ideas, legislative efforts, and program implementation do not mean a thing if the time is not right. For example, U.S. business firms interested in developing commercial relations with the People's Republic of China (PRC) should have been making inquiries in Washington when it became apparent that the Carter administration intended to normalize diplomatic relations with the PRC. Many good ideas never become legislation because the timing is not right. A good lobbyist knows when to act on an idea whose time has come. Success follows when the lobbyist knows the right time to act. It is not sufficient to be informed about the mechanics of Congress, the White House, or the regulatory agencies; any political science professor has this information. Timing can be everything in selling an idea.

Finally, to lobby effectively, the lobbyist must be trustworthy.

In the action-oriented world of Washington, trust is often accepted as a substitute for factual verification. Commissioners, congressmen, and agency department heads are asked to make many policy decisions each day. Often the only basis for their decisions is short discussions with lobbyists. Certain lobbyists, be they on the White House congressional relations staff or employed by public or private special interest groups and trade associations, have come to be accepted as the Washington equivalent of the Delphic oracle. Their success is based on an open and frank discussion of an issue, even though in a particular situation the decision may go against them. Their constant willingness to discuss all sides of an issue guarantees access. Access represents power, and in Washington access is based on trust.

If a business firm wishes to hire a lobbyist or lobby on its own, it is important to know that the most successful lobbyists in Washington depend upon a coterie of experts—lawyers, accountants, economists, and former government officials and military officers. Robert R. Nathan Associates, Charls E. Walker Associates, and Timmons and Company are three of the more important Washington lobbying firms. These firms are filled with former high government officials who know how to get things done and when to make the right moves. For example, when Chrysler needed the support of the president and Congress for the financial bailout, it called on Timmons and Company to lead its efforts. It might be added that Price Waterhouse has an Office of Government Services in Washington that was created to help bring business and government together on issues of mutual interest.

In 1974, the Federal Election Commission ruled that corporations—forbidden by law to make direct political contributions—could set up political action committees (PACs), like those of labor unions, and solicit campaign funds from employees. Business PACs have increased from 89 in 1974 to 1226 in 1980. In the 1978 congressional elections, the business PACs raised $22 million for candidates friendly to the interests of business. Contributions from the business PACs are expected to increase in 1980. There is concern in Congress over the growing power of the business PACs, and efforts are being made to restrict the amounts they can give to any one candidate. The machinists' union recently filed a complaint with the Federal Election Commission, charging some corporations and business groups with using threats and intimidation to extract donations from employees. Among the corporations accused were General Electric, General Motors, and Standard Oil of Indiana.

A troika of congressional members and their staffs, executive officials, and lobbyists is a common Washington phenomenon. They are typically bound together by a subject of mutual interest—taxes, foreign trade, and so forth. The three groups come to know, trust, and depend upon each other for support and assistance. As part of this troika, a lobbyist becomes privy to draft proposals, new ideas, and the current Washington gossip. He or she may assist in the development of regulations, legislation, and proposed ideas for action. This role is often developed over time through a close working relationship with people of similar interests. A corporation or trade association may hire as a lobbyist a person who is part of this troika, for example, a legislative staff member or former congressman, thus creating automatic access to the remaining members of the troika for the lobbyist's employer. In any case, the three-cornered relationship is important, and a lobbyist who is a part of the relationship is better able to perform the lobbying function.

Public Opinion as a Lobbying Tool

H. L. Mencken once said, "Never overestimate the intelligence of the American public." [14] Decision makers pay attention to public opinion and listen to what pollsters and other public opinion samplers have to say about what the public is thinking. In fact, one gets the impression that President Carter conducted domestic economic policy, foreign policy, and his political strategy on the basis of what his pollster, Pat Caddell, found out from his polling of public opinion. Elected officials in Congress also rely on public opinion polls as a vital part of their continuing efforts to remain in office. They rely not only upon the regular syndicated polls carried out by the Lou Harris and Gallup organizations, which are applicable to the general public as a whole, but also utilize their own pollsters to sample constituent opinion. Sometimes these polls are very limited in scope and reliability, particularly when they are done by the legislator rather than a professional pollster. Local newspapers may also use public opinion polls, but their accuracy may be limited by the use of unreliable sampling techniques.

Organizations such as Common Cause, the U.S. Chamber of Commerce, and the National Rifle Association take polls and make the results available to decision makers. Generally the results are based on tabulations of questionnaires returned by a portion of the organization's members, and a bias is automatically built in. However, congressmen will pay attention to the polls, particularly if they are made by an organization to which they are allied. Thus public opinion, as expressed through the medium of polling, can be an effective lobbying tool. A lobbyist can use public opinion as an effective backup in support of a position, for it establishes a certain legitimacy about the position. After all, the public supports it, not just some selfish special interest group. Public opinion is a barometer for Washington lobbying, and as a barometer it indicates the ups and downs of citizen sentiments. Rarely do public opinion polls spell out a course of action; they indicate direction but provide little information on how to get there.

14

Going to the Bank: Personalities and Debts

THE AFFABLE THOMAS HALE BOGGS, partner in the Washington law firm of Patton, Boggs, and Blow, is regarded as one of the most successful lawyer-lobbyists in Washington. Since both his father and mother represented a Louisiana district in Congress for a number of years, he comes by his Washington acumen naturally. Boggs states that knowledge of the personalities involved in any given issue is basic to success in achieving your goal. It is also important to know how particular legislators or bureaucrats act and react on issues; this information is not usually available in print.[1] To know legislators and bureaucrats is a key factor in building obligations that can be banked at appropriate times. The old adage, "It's not what you know, but who you know that counts," is quite relevant to the Washington scene. A quid pro quo relationship is created by successful lawyers, lobbyists, and other contact persons by helping, trusting, and knowing the right government officials.

The backgrounds and attitudes of government people—congressmen and their staffs, the president and his staff, commissioners, and ranking bureaucrats—are indicators of where they stand politically, economically, and socially on given issues and of how they might act in a particular situation. John T. Dunlop, secretary of labor during the Ford administration, makes the point that businessmen and people in government differ in many respects.

> They have different backgrounds, approach issues with different time horizons, see the press and other media in quite different roles, and they have quite different institutional objectives and—at times—different personal values. Furthermore, each group sees the role of the law in society in substantially different ways—government, to change; business, largely to preserve. The businessman's perspective often tends to be international, while the government administrator's is much more narrowly national. The two groups are often separated by a gap in age and experience.[2]

Government officials and business executives are constantly thrown into contact with each other, typically in adversary positions. Because of differing backgrounds and goals, they find it difficult to communicate, much less agree about difficult substantive issues and values. The absence of business leadership on many public policy issues has meant that business has forfeited input almost entirely to bureaucrats and politicians. Business interests do not have an effective mechanism or procedure to reconcile their conflicting interests on a wide variety of public policy issues. On the government side, there has been a rapid expansion of government regulation and with it a government penchant for rigid bureaucratic command and control regulations, even when these are ineffective and counterproductive.[3] As society becomes more complex there is a need for the skills and qualities of business executives. There is also a need for business executives and government administrators to understand not only the substantive issues of key areas of government activity and joint decision-making, but also to understand the constraints and settings in which the other operates.

Personality of Government

The late lyricist Johnny Mercer wrote a song called "Personality" in which the success of the great femmes fatales of history (such as Salome and Madame Pompadour) was attributed to what was euphemistically called their "personality." But the word *personality,* as it will be used here, refers to a set of characteristics that include age, sex, party affiliation, schooling, career pattern, values, and established and unestablished policy positions. These characteristics can give a clue as to how an individual or group of individuals will react in a given situation. For example, Irving Shapiro, chairman of the board of duPont and a member of the Business Roundtable, states that business leaders have learned that to understand federal government tax policy it is necessary to understand the personality of Senator Russell Long, chairman of the Senate Finance Committee. To know an official and to be able to talk with him or her is important, but successful lobbyists also know what approach will pay off with that person. Choosing the right approach is determined by the following factors.

Age

It was noted in an earlier chapter that congressional staffs are generally young, particularly House staffs. The electoral revolution of the 1970s resulted in the election of younger senators and representatives. The members of the personal staff of the president tend to be younger than businessmen with comparable responsibility. (Hamilton Jordan and Jody Powell, for example, are in their mid-thirties.) This has not always been the case. The Eisenhower administration can be contrasted with the Carter administration in terms of age and performance of the White House staffs. Most of the Eisenhower staff had had previous business and government experience. Sherman Adams, for example, was a former governor of New Hampshire. Carter appointees to various agencies and commissions were also younger than those appointed by Eisenhower and Kennedy. It is not unusual today for a senior corporate vice-president who is fifty-five to discuss an issue with a congressional staff member who is thirty-three. This scenario is repeated throughout Washington every day in many situations.

Sex

Most senior government officials in Washington are male, as are their business counterparts. Through affirmative action policies, efforts have been made in recent years to increase the number of women in senior government positions. Two women were appointed to cabinet positions by President Carter. On Capitol Hill, the number of women legislators now stands at twenty-one, with Nancy Kassebaum and Paula Hawkins as Senators from Kansas and Florida, respectively, and nineteen women serving in the House. The majority of senior staff members—administrative assistants, legislative assistants, and committee counsels—are men. However, there is a greater turnover in senior government positions than there is in business, and it is likely that more women will be involved in the policy-making decisions of government in the future. This could mean that corporate males will increasingly come face-to-face with female government policymakers.

Party Affiliation

Party affiliation is of importance to the election or appointment of certain government officials, but is of far less importance in dealing with bureaucracy and the regulatory commissions. After the elections are over, party affiliation takes a backseat to political philosophy. There is the conservative coalition, comprised of many Republicans and southern Democrats. There are some Democrats who have a more conservative voting record than most Republicans. By the same token, there is compatibility between liberal Democrats and liberal Republicans. There are trade-offs between members of both political parties, and favors pass back and forth. An elemental maxim is "You scratch my back, and I will scratch your back." A practical rule for business firms that wish to contribute money to political campaigns is to help friends in both parties. Also be aware of the limited party patronage available, if patronage is a goal. Patronage and party affiliation are used to fill certain jobs on Capitol Hill, high-level jobs in the bureaucracy and regulatory commissions, and some diplomatic positions.

People who get these positions are usually long-time faithful party workers and financial contributors.

School Ties

Schools attended can make a difference in terms of entry into some government positions. For example, graduates of Georgetown University's international relations program have an advantage for admission into the U.S. foreign service. Harvard and Yale law graduates are in demand on Capitol Hill. However, school ties probably mean much less today than they meant twenty years ago. It used to be that attendance at Exeter, Andover, and Groton, and Harvard, Yale, and Princeton could automatically parlay a person into a position with the State Department. A conduit from the Ivy League schools was maintained through an "old boy" network, but this is no longer the case. The school attended makes little difference after entry into Washington circles has been achieved. Many of the Carter people were products of the University of Georgia. It is of some importance to at least be aware of the fact that some government people respond better to persons with similar educational training—lawyers to lawyers, engineers to engineers, and schools to schools.

Careers

Very few government employees have had any business background. This includes senators and representatives. On Capitol Hill less than 4 percent of committee and subcommittee staff members have business backgrounds. Most of the senior bureaucrats have had no business experience. This fact illustrates a fundamental problem in the area of government and business relations: The two sides simply do not understand each other. The career patterns of business executives and government administrators and legislators are totally different. An abrasive interface has developed over time, with government cast in the role of Robin Hood by its defenders and business put in the role of the Sheriff of Nottingham by its detractors. But this government-business dichotomy appears to be chang-

ing as business becomes more successful in articulating its positions. A contrast has developed between the poorly informed,
narrow interests of some business groups and a well-informed
connection to a broader interest used by other business groups.
But there still remains a critical gap in communication between
business executives and government officials.

Washington probably has more lawyers per capita than any
other city in the world. Nearly 40,000 lawyers work in the
Washington area, with 8,000 of them employed by the federal
government in one capacity or another. Thousands of other
lawyers specialize in helping clients to advance their interests
before the various agencies of the federal government. Much
of what they do is not easily recognized as practicing law. They
educate their clients about how a bill becomes law, the politics
of regulatory commissions, or the significance of White House
executive orders. In the executive branch of government, lawyers are very much involved in policymaking. Of President
Carter's thirteen cabinet members, eight were lawyers. Each, in
turn, relied on a general counsel, who may employ hundreds
of assistants for legal and policy advice on an array of issues. In
addition, in every major agency and regulatory commission
lawyers occupy many nonlegal positions. The end result of lawyer dominance is that no decision, no legislative proposal, no
regulation, no contract, and no move to crack down on law
violators can develop without the approval of one or more government attorneys.[4]

It used to be that the legal profession was an almost automatic requirement for entrance into politics. Although the importance of law as a political requisite has declined over time,
over half of the senators and representatives in Congress today
have legal backgrounds. For example, in the Louisiana delegation to Congress, both senators and five of the eight representatives were lawyers before their election to Congress.[5] In the
ninety-fifth Congress, 68 of the 100 senators were lawyers by
profession, compared with 24 businessmen and bankers.[6]
Members of Congress also employ lawyers on their personal
staffs and on the numerous congressional committees and subcommittees. It is argued by critics of Congress that it does not
reflect a true socioeconomic composite of the population of the

United States. For one thing, there are too many lawyers and not enough members from other occupations. Rarely does a member of Congress emerge from a trade union or a so-called blue collar occupation. Most legislators are male, well-educated, middle-aged, and from middle- or upper-middle-income backgrounds. Until recently, a majority were also WASPS—white Anglo-Saxon Protestants.[7]

Political Values

There are two different value systems in political Washington—freedom of enterprise and egalitarianism. Other terms can be used: an individualistic ethic as opposed to a communitarian ethic, equality of opportunity versus equality of result, and meritocracy versus equality. The supporters of free enterprise want government to do less; egalitarians want government to do more, particularly in the area of social welfare. As mentioned previously, freedom of enterprise and individualism are supposed to be consistent with the principles of a free society in that they carry with them the concepts of freedom to live and work as one prefers and to enjoy the fruits of one's labor. Through energy applied to the fulfillment of personal needs, the individual pushes society forward. In a free enterprise market economy, an allocation of earned rewards and income is implicit in the system.

The proponents of egalitarianism have constructed a complex redistribution system based on welfare and other related programs tiered on one another and permeating all levels of government. A large cadre of professionals in various agencies is responsible for deciding who gets the tax dollars—the elderly, veterans, farmers, poor people, minorities, and so forth. The Department of Health and Human Resources and the Veterans Administration oversee the redistribution of billions of dollars annually. Sociologist Robert Nisbet refers to these and other agencies as examples of what he calls the "new despotism," and notes, "If we plot the development of social equality in Western society over the past few centuries, we find it follows almost perfectly the development of centralization and bureaucratization in the political sphere."[8] The famous economist Friedrich Hayek makes a similar point in *The Road to Serfdom,* in which individuals become the serfs and centralized bureaucracy in the welfare state becomes the lord of the manor.[9] There is indeed a large number of government officials who feel that government alone can provide the answers to all social problems.

Sociologist Amitai Etzioni has made the point that America is now in the position of having to opt for one of two choices: a reindustrialized society or a society that stresses leisure and what some people refer to as the "quality of life." [10] The first option places emphasis on cutting back not only government spending but also private consumption in order to provide funds to build up the infrastructure and capital goods sectors of the economy. The motivation to work, which has weakened in American society, would have to be strengthened. The second option involves preoccupation with self and more communing with nature. This option, Etzioni fears, would create a society with less drive and productivity, with the result that the United States would lose its economic strength and become a "siesta society" like some of the South American countries. The loss of productive capacity, which is a major contributor to inflation, can be cured only through austerity; this means that various segments of society would have to learn to live with less rather than more.

Family Life

The recent movie *The Seduction of Joe Tynan* is not too far off in depicting the lives of many of Washington's politicians. In the film, Alan Alda, who portrays a liberal senator from an eastern state, is seduced (actually) by lawyer-lobbyist Meryl Streep, and figuratively by his own political ambitions. He is alienated from his wife, and his children do not know who he is. Family life does take a beating in Washington, particularly among elected politicians. The divorce rate is high for politicians, but perhaps not higher than the rate for the nation as a whole. Congressmen often retire because their jobs place too many constraints on family life. But there are those who enjoy living in Washington and being a part of the power structure. Wives and children can often be close confidants and advisors to government officials. Rosalynn Carter, considered by some observers to be an eminence grise, or power behind the throne, undoubtedly played a strong advisory role to the president. Contacts may be created by knowing the spouses and relatives of those in power.

How to Build Up a Debt

Congressmen, the president and his cabinet, commissioners, and bureaucrats have many demands placed on them. One demand is allegiance to a political party—attending meetings, speaking at political banquets, and so forth. Constituents also place a demand on time: A congressman must please the voters, and Health and Human Resources bureaucrats must satisfy the claims of constituent groups such as the poor and the elderly. The president must run the country, satisfy his constituencies, campaign for members of his own party, and engage in other political activities. Congressmen must debate and vote, serve on committees and subcommittees, and research issues. Social activities, such as attending the annual convention of the Alfalfa Growers Association of America, are a part of time constraints. Finally, there is the family, which also places a demand upon the time of legislators and bureaucrats.

It is necessary to build up a debt by helping a congressman or bureaucrat meet these demands. Most people in Washington will remember those persons who have been helpful. To build up a debt, it is important to know something about the person involved—age, political party, schooling, family, membership in fraternal organizations, and other reference points. The next step is to provide assistance in some capacity: help in a political campaign, support the political party, assist in constituent service, write statements, provide help to family, and so forth. Be a trusted and loyal supporter, but also be candid, even though it may appear to be against your interest in the short run. The best way to gain access to the Washington scene is to provide some form of useful assistance to key people.

Government: It Is People, Too!

People make up government, not the Washington Monument, the White House, or the Capitol. Knowing who these people are, how they communicate, the activities they perform, and the rules of the game by which they play is important. Generally, government people with influence in Washington are male, white, middle to upper-middle class, and college educated. Communication by congressional staffs tends to be largely among themselves, their bosses, and their bosses' constituents. A broad range of intensity and specialization of activity exists among people in government. Some of the most active and least specialized persons include senior staff members of the Executive Office of the President and the congressional committees, whereas experts are found in the bureaucracy and regulatory commissions.

The activities and behavior of people in government can be explained in terms of attributes and environments. It is perhaps of some importance to know that Senator Jack Danforth is a Yale graduate, an ordained Episcopal minister, and an heir to the Ralston-Purina fortune. It also may be of importance to know that bureaucrats outnumber congressional staff by a ratio of nearly 100 to 1, and President Reagan's staff by a ratio of 700 to 1. These facts mean little if they cannot be used systematically to attain an end. There are certain questions that facts can help answer. For example, what do we need to know about Commissioner X's experience and personality? To whom does he or she talk? No book, library, data bank, or consultant can provide all the answers. It is possible to better pursue an objective by knowing the answers to personality questions, no matter how trivial, and then acting in a timely manner with the answers.

15

A Final Perspective on Business-Government Relations

MANY DIVERSE GROUPS operate in Washington. This is apparent when one takes a tour of the area around the White House. For example, there is the U.S. Chamber of Commerce almost across the street from the White House, and just around the corner on Sixteenth Street is the headquarters of the AFL-CIO, with a beautiful mosaic in the lobby. If one walks up Sixteenth Street to K Street, the United Mine Workers building is on the left down one block, and at Sixteenth and M Streets are the National Education Association and the American Chemical Society buildings. The headquarters of the National Rifle Association is where Sixteenth Street runs into Scott Circle. What you have then are groups ranging from the Chamber of Commerce to the National Rifle Association, all with their self-interest in mind and all operating in Washington. Some of the groups measure success in terms of votes, others in terms of acres of forest land preserved or snail darters saved from speedboats and coyotes from traps. Washington is the home of over 1,400 trade associations, dozens of unions, hundreds of lobbyists, and thousands of lawyers, all working on behalf of one special interest group or another.

Opponents of Business

To paraphrase an often-heard quote from the movie *Star Wars,* the Force is not necessarily with you. Although business has done a more effective job in recent years in getting out of the boardroom into the Washington political arena, gains can be lost. One basic law to remember when working in Washington is never assume that the other side is sitting still. There are too many competing interest groups, some of which have no love for business. One such group, coordinated by self-anointed consumer advocates, antibusiness union officials, and social activists, aims to curb the power of business in the United States. The group is headed by the grand panjandrum of all the social reformers, Ralph Nader. April 17, 1980, was designated by Nader as Big Business Day, a day designed to celebrate the contributions of American business to society by focusing attention on so-called corporate crimes—tyranny, corruption, and so forth. The long-range objective of Nader's Big Business Day is the Corporate Democracy Act, sponsored, of course, by Nader and his minions, and aimed at democratizing business by creating corporate boards made up completely of consumer and labor interests.

"Sentence first, verdict afterwards," said the Red Queen to Alice.[1] Business is guilty and must be punished, say Ralph Nader and his cohorts. Never mind taking an objective look at the American economic system, and forget the fact that Russian consumers have to queue up for up to six hours to buy meat and other products that may be unavailable by the time they reach the head of the line. Moreover, the price of meat, if there is any, is $50 a pound. Also forget the fact that the two most viable economies in the world, Japan and West Germany, have far less government regulation of business than the United States. However, noise, protest, and a scattering of famous names lend remarkable credibility to any movement, so business cannot afford to be complacent about the future. It has too much at stake and must do a better job of selling the contributions of American business and the market economy—contributions that are impossible under centralized government planning.

In a recent article in *Time* magazine, entitled "The Corporate Chief's New Class," Irving Shapiro, chairman of duPont, is quoted as follows:

> It is startling how much corporate America has changed. In the past, businessmen wore blinders. After hours, they would run to their club, play golf with other businessmen, have a martini, and that was about it. They did not see their role as being concerned with public policy issues. In a world where government simply took taxes from you and did not interfere with your operations, maybe that idea was sensible. In today's world, it is not. I'm much more interested in what Russell Long thinks than what some businessman thinks. And you can find out from Russell Long very simply what he thinks.[2]

He is quite right. Corporate America, with some exceptions, has changed. There is much more awareness of what is going on in the world, particularly the government world, and more of a willingness to get involved in policy issues. But Shapiro and other business leaders hold out no false hopes that business will be loved or become a popular force in this country. There are too many opposing groups for this to happen, and it is possible that federal legislation regulating business will increase in the future. The goal of business, according to Shapiro, is to create an arm's-length but nonadversary relationship between business and government. Business must be involved in solving problems, and government should exploit the talents of business people. It is important for business to be able to relate to the real world, which includes dealing with government as an institution. Shapiro states that if he were choosing a chief executive, relating to the larger world would be of more importance than knowing how to produce widgets.

Where Does Business Go from Here?

The business-government milieu has been altered dramatically during this century as the United States has been transformed from a capitalist economy into a hybrid or mixed economy composed of private enterprise, public enterprise, and joint public-private enterprise. Almost every business decision is affected by the laws, regulations, or voluntary guidelines of some level of government. There was the time when Franklin D. Roosevelt was roundly cussed and discussed by corporate executives from Bangor, Maine, to San Luis Obispo, California, but what he did to change the business-government interface was mild compared with what happened to business during the 1970s. This decade witnessed a vast expansion of the scope and detail of government regulation of business that surpassed anything that happened during the New Deal period. New federal agencies were created to regulate such areas as consumer product safety, occupational safety, and protection of the environment, and old agencies, such as the Federal Trade Commission and the Securities and Exchange Commission, were given additional power to investigate and regulate business. Litigation against business by special interest groups has increased the involvement of the courts, and congressional committees and their staffs have developed the power to hold up private business decisions for scrutiny and review.

Probably the most dramatic recent event is the federal government's attempt to bail out Chrysler. Since the days of Adam Smith, economists have maintained that business failure is essential to the smooth operation of a market economy. Eliminating failure as an option would seriously disrupt the functioning of the market. The late Harvard economist Joseph Schumpeter argued that it was only through a cleansing of the economy to eliminate inefficient, noninnovative producers that a nation could reach its full growth potential. To put it more succinctly, the possibility of bankruptcy is a necessary incentive for efficiency. However, despite the many economic arguments against providing financial support to insolvent or inefficient firms, assistance in the form of loan guarantees was provided to Chrysler, perhaps creating a precedent for the creation of another Reconstruction Finance Corporation to ensure that financially troubled companies will not go broke waiting in line for Congress to hand out aid. This would interpose further the role of the federal government in the marketplace by making it a lender of last resort that would protect the inefficient at the expense of the efficient.

Political Involvement

The Chrysler bailout is attributed by Ralph Nader and others to the political machinations of big business. However, it is more likely that the United Auto Workers had more say in the bailout. It is unlikely that Congress would take the trouble to help Chrysler save Lee Iacocca's job. Nevertheless, business involvement in the political decision-making process has increased considerably, beginning in the middle 1970s with the creation of a number of political action committees (PACs). The recurrent congressional fight over legislation determining the powers of the Federal Trade Commission has become the strongest reflection of the new-found strength of business, not only with its traditional political ally, the Republican party, but also with the Democratic party. Essential elements in the politicization of business were the formation in 1972 of the Business Roundtable, which represents the elite of the corporate community, the revitalization of the Chamber of Commerce, and the conversion of the National Federation of Independent Businessmen (NFIB) into an effective lobbying instrument. The NFIB has 596,000 members who contribute between $30 and $500, based on a willingness to pay, exclusively for political leverage in Washington and in some state capitals.

The political involvement of business is decried by other interest groups. It can be argued, however, that "What is sauce for the goose is sauce for the gander." For many years, special interest groups—unions, consumerists, and environmentalists—had their own way in Washington. Business had little input into the decision-making process, and a number of laws were passed directly affecting business without any business input. There was a time when Ralph Nader probably had more clout with Congress than the entire business community of the United States. Laws were passed that were extremely costly to business. They were poorly designed by people who knew nothing and cared nothing about business. So business became politicized, and corporate executives no longer could afford the luxury of damning the federal government at Rotary clubs and country clubs as their predecessors did during the Roosevelt days. The phenomenal growth of corporate and trade association PACs, while significant, became equaled in importance by the extensive politicization of corporate officials running the gamut from small-town car dealers through the middle- and upper-echelon executives of multinational corporations.

However, some reaction has set in against business lobbying. As can be expected, criticism comes from Nader, who accuses business of exercising veto control over Congress. More important criticism comes from other sources. The practice of turning business employees into letter writers to Congress supporting business causes is criticized by some as arm-twisting. Civil libertarians complain that it is an invasion of privacy. While corporations that sponsor letter-writing campaigns stress that participation is voluntary, even voluntary action must be motivated. Congress has become aware of the quantum increase in company-inspired mail and is likely to pay less attention to it in the future. Moreover, it is entirely conceivable that it may legislate this type of political approach. Congressman Frank Thompson introduced a bill to give the National Labor Relations Board jurisdiction over supervisory employees, a first step toward the protection of all employees from political arm-twisting.

It may be advisable for business to be a little more circumspect in its political involvement, particularly with respect to employee participation. The question of whether business ought to play an important role in the political process is one of increasing concern to both business and the public. A dilemma has developed with respect to business involvement in politics: As it becomes increasingly successful in winning its legislative battles, the public becomes more distrustful. It is argued that as members of the House and Senate are increasingly unable to depend on local political organizations for direction on key issues before Congress, the ability to persuade even a small percentage of the business community to make its view known carries enormous weight and is a key factor in the changing of the ideological tone of Congress. Other interest groups complain that business has the financial clout to exercise leverage on Congress. The public is generally receptive to this complaint because of the long-standing poor image of big business. There are also those who feel that the increased influence of pressure groups constitutes a danger to the whole process of government.

A recent article in the *Harvard Business Review* makes the point that if business is to maintain or enhance its political position in the future, it must take the following steps:

1. Recognize that the political power now held by business is not permanent, and that it will take care, skill, and effort even to maintain the current level of influence in the future.
2. Create a set of political activity guidelines that meet both the legal and moral standards of our society.
3. Establish an effective political activity control system within individual companies or industries before outside groups legislate one.
4. Train managers in the political arena, since this should help reduce their anxiety about political risk-taking.
5. Take the general public's interest into account equally with corporate needs when formulating a political position.[3]

The article, which involved polling the extent of business participation in politics, goes on to make the point that there is a desire and a need on the part of management to be more effective in the political decision-making process.[4] To some extent there was a feeling that it is necessary to inform society that its long-term interests and those of business are similar. It was recognized that business should take a more intelligent and open-minded position on issues, and that there is a need to improve the image of business. There was an increase in the use of lobbyists in Washington and in the employment of specialists to deal with government officials. Executives polled felt that there could be continued political activity on the part of business in the future, and that this was necessary because government is the core in which decisions affecting business are made. To ignore this fact is to invite disaster; executives need the same access points to government decision-making that are available to leaders of other interest groups. If nothing else, political action by business provides a balance to political action by unions.

The public, however, is not very sanguine about the role of business in the political decision-making process. For example, executives in the poll saw increased political action by unions as justification for increased business political action by a ratio of 7 to 1, while the public in the poll agreed with this justification by a ratio of only 2 to 1.[5] A majority of the public sampled in the poll felt that business involvement in the political process should be less extensive in the future. What this may mean is that certain types of political action should be continued by business, but excessive political action, particularly on the part of the larger corporations, may not be wise because a negative climate will be created that will affect all business firms. There are too many groups that are hostile to the interests of business to run the risk of increased control by Congress of the political actions of business.

The Business-Government Interface of the Future

In 1887 Edward Bellamy published his utopian novel *Looking Backward,* in which the protagonist is hypnotized in an attempt to cure his insomnia, but through accident remains in a state of suspended animation for a period of 113 years, until he is discovered and awakened.[6] The changes that have occurred over the period are tremendous. In the novel, 1887 saw the concentration of business into the hands of fewer and fewer firms, small business firms were failing rapidly, and the chain stores were beginning to crush the country stores. Moreover, enormous inequalities in the distribution of income and wealth had also developed. The concentration of business, income, and wealth continued until people realized they must do something to protect themselves from exploitation, and since they recognized that breaking up the trusts and returning to small-scale enterprise would be inefficient, they took over the control of industry and commerce for themselves.

In the year 2000, all industry is nationalized, and all citizens between the ages of twenty-one and forty-five are required to serve in the industrial army. No wages are paid, but all citizens, be they active or retired, receive equal shares in the national income. At the beginning of each year, every citizen is given a credit card marked off in dollars and cents, and every time he or she makes a purchase the amount is punched out of this card. If there is any surplus at the end of the year, it may be used the following year or returned to a common fund. All consumer goods are of the best quality, since there is no point in the people cheating themselves by making inferior goods. There are no federal, state, or local debts; no army and navy; no internal revenue service, because there are no taxes; and no money. In the absence of money, the incentives that impel workers to do their best are patriotism, prizes, and so forth. If any person who is capable of work refuses to do it, he or she may find himself or herself in solitary confinement on bread and water.

With less than twenty years to go in this century, it is not likely that the United States will achieve the state of grace visualized in Bellamy's industrialized society of the future, nor is this a tragedy. It is also unlikely that the United States will reach the state-controlled and -regulated society envisioned by George Orwell in his novel *1984,* with group think and the ubiquitous "Big Brother is Watching" slogan. However, the country appears to be in the process of undergoing some sort of transformation that will undoubtedly have a considerable impact upon business. What direction this transformation will take is difficult to ascertain, for we are living in an age of uncertainty, and our value system is in a state of flux. One has to be endowed with a certain amount of prescience to be able to predict what American society will be like in 1990, much less in the year 2000; in the absence of prescience, the only thing that can be done is to try to review some of the forces that may affect business during the 1980s.

There are those who have an apocalyptic view of the 1980s. A recent *Business Week* article was titled "A Shrinking Standard of Living." [7] Its premise was that the golden age of the consumer is over, and the U.S. standard of living is declining. There will be inflation and increased political and social tensions over a smaller economic pie. This could lead to increased tensions between labor and management. The rate of economic growth will decline, and there will be less real disposable income available for discretionary purchases. This decline in living standards can be attributed to a number of factors, not the least of which is high-priced oil, but high-priced oil cannot be made the villain in the set piece. There has been a national malaise of leadership accompanied by a lack of purpose. Competing special interest groups impose a variety of claims upon the national economy, unions want more wages, the elderly want higher pensions, farmers want greater subsidies, and so forth. Pandora's box, once opened, is difficult to close.

"Optimism," said a character in one of Voltaire's plays, "is a mania for maintaining that all is well when things are going badly." [8] There does not appear to be much room for optimism, with inflation becoming a hallmark of life and American industry taking a beating in international competition. It was noted in a lead article in *Business Week,* titled "U.S. Autos: Losing a Big Segment of the Market Forever?" [9] that foreign automobile companies have taken over an increasingly larger segment of the U.S. domestic market. By the end of 1980 the Japanese are expected to be the world's largest producers of automobiles, further cutting the share now held by U.S. auto firms, and both Chrysler and Ford are expected to lose money. The opening words of an International Workers of the World song of the 1920s, "Times are getting hard, boys; money is getting scarce," are as relevant to the United States today as they were then.

The projected problems of the 1980s should call for closer cooperation between business and government and less of the abrasive interface that has existed over the last forty years. Skillful and creative leadership will be needed to provide solutions to the economic and social problems of this decade. The tension between economic efficiency and political equity will have to be reduced in favor of mutual cooperation between business and government. Executives will have to leave their personal politics and biases at home and learn to work better with people in government. The same holds true of government. Then, too, the relationship between business and government is so totally different in this country than it is in Japan and Western Europe: adversary as opposed to cooperation. With the Japanese providing ever-stronger competition, it is necessary to rethink the business-government role in the United States.

Notes

Notes

Chapter 1. The Political Marketplace (pp. 1–14)

1. William De Lancey, president, Republic Steel Corporation, "The Federal Presence in Steel." Speech delivered at Cold Finished Bar Institute Annual Meeting, Washington, D.C., December 4, 1975, pp. 2–3.
2. U.S. Congress, Joint Economic Committee, *The 1979 Economic Report of the President,* January 1979, p. 32.
3. U.S. Congress, Joint Economic Committee, *Productivity in the Federal Government,* May 31, 1979, pp. 1–11.

Chapter 2. The Cost of Regulation (pp. 15–24)

1. U.S. Congress, Joint Economic Committee, *Hearings on the 1979 Economic Report of the President,* 1979.
2. *The Costs of Government Regulation of Business,* study prepared for the Subcommittee on Economic Growth and Stabilization, 1978.
3. U.S. Commission on Federal Paperwork, *Annual Report 1977,* p. 8.

4. "Dow Chemical's Catalog of Regulatory Horrors," *Business Week,*
   April 4, 1977, p. 50. Also, "The Impact of Government Regulation on the Dow Chemical Company" (Midland, Michigan: Dow
   Chemical), pamphlet.
5. U.S. Council on Environmental Quality, *Fourth Annual Report,*
   December 1973, p. 93.
6. "Can Chrysler Be Saved?," *Newsweek,* August 13, 1979.
7. U.S. Occupational Safety and Health Administration, *Annual Report 1977,* p. 12.
8. Murray L. Weidenbaum, *Government-Mandated Price Increases*
   (Washington: American Enterprise Institute, 1975), p. 26.
9. Ibid., p. 26.
10. *Business Week,* March 12, 1979, pp. 74–82.
11. *Time,* August 27, 1979, p. 36.
12. U.S. Congress, Joint Economic Committee, *The 1978 Midyear Re-
    view of the Economy,* part 2, p. 298.
13. William W. Lockwood, *The State and Economic Enterprise in Japan*
    (Princeton: Princeton University Press, 1965).
14. For a comprehensive discussion of the Japanese tax system, see
    An Outline of Japanese Taxes, published annually by the Japanese
    Ministry of Finance. It is in English.
15. American antitrust laws rest in part on the belief that competition
    is an effective regulator of most markets and, with a few excep-
    tions, that monopolistic practices can be stopped by competition.
16. Martin C. Schnitzer, *Contemporary Government and Business Rela-
    tions* (Chicago: Rand McNally, 1978), pp. 245–251.
17. Jean Jacques Servan-Schreiber, *The American Challenge* (New
    York: Atheneum, 1968).
18. I noted with considerable interest the treatment of some Japa-
    nese businessmen in Poland. They were met at the airport by
    representatives of the Japanese embassy in Warsaw, taken
    through customs, driven through Poland by embassy officials,
    and delivered to the airport.

Chapter 3. The Second Managerial Revolution (pp. 25–35)

1. Murray L. Weidenbaum, *Government-Mandated Price Increases*
   (Washington: American Enterprise Institute, 1975), p. 88.

2. Adolf A. Berle and Gardiner C. Means, *The Modern Corporation and Private Property,* rev. ed. (New York: Harcourt Brace Jovanovich, 1968).

3. The concept of social Darwinism was developed by the English philosopher Herbert Spenser. His disciples in the United States were William Graham Sumner and John B. Clark. Sumner, a professor of moral philosophy at Yale, had a particularly strong impact on American thought.

4. Council on Environmental Quality, *Eighth Annual Report,* December 1977, pp. 224–231.

5. The case of Comstock v. General Motors disclosed the fact that the Buick Roadmaster had a defective power brake system, and General Motors had to issue two separate kits for the replacement of separate parts.

6. The consumer protection powers of the Federal Trade Commission were extended by the Consumer Product Warranty Act. Title II of the act amends the original Federal Trade Commission Act to read "in or affecting commerce," in place of simply "in commerce."

7. The AT&T case is a prime example of restitution. AT&T has had to pay out around $75 million in restitution to groups that the government said had been victims of discrimination.

8. Daniel Bell, "On Meritocracy and Equality," *The Public Interest,* no. 29, Fall 1972, pp. 18–32.

9. Griggs v. Duke Power Co., 401 U.S. 424 (1971). Under the general guidelines of Griggs v. Duke Power, no question may be asked either in a preemployment application or of a prospective applicant that does not have a clear business necessity.

10. U.S. Chamber of Commerce, Antitrust Task Force on International Trade and Investment, *Final Report on U.S. Antitrust and American Exports,* 1974.

11. James Q. Wilson, "The Dead Hand of Regulation," *The Public Interest,* no. 25, Fall 1971, pp. 20–35.

12. Ralph Nader, *Taming the Giant Corporation* (New York: W. W. Norton, 1976).

13. Ibid., pp. 207–210; also Donald E. Schwartz, "Federal Chartering of Corporations: An Introduction," *Georgetown Law Review,* vol. 72, 1972, pp. 72–73.

14. This is discussed in Chapter 7, "How Laws Are Passed."

15. James W. Singer, "Business and Government: A New 'Quasi-Public' Role," *National Journal,* April 4, 1978, p. 596.

16. H. Igor Ansoff, "The State of Practice in Planning Systems," *Sloan Management Review,* vol. 18, no. 2, Winter 1977, p. 3.

Chapter 4. Business as Advocate (pp. 36–54)

1. Matthew Josephson, *The Robber Barons* (New York: Harcourt, Brace, & World, 1934).
2. *Roanoke Times,* October 24, 1975, p. 8.
3. *Washington Post,* November 8, 1974, p. 3.
4. Harry Williams, *Huey Long* (New York: Alfred A. Knopf, 1969), p. 416.
5. There have already been bills introduced to regulate the oil industry. For example, the Petroleum Industry Bill of 1975 would have required the eighteen largest oil companies to reduce their operations to one activity, either production, transportation, refining, or marketing. Similar bills have been introduced in Congress since 1975. The Energy Deconcentration Act proposes to fragment the industry both horizontally and vertically. The scope of operation of any one firm would be limited to one of four activities: production, refining, transportation, or marketing.
6. U.S. Congress, Senate, Committee on Foreign Relations, *Multinational Corporations and United States Foreign Policy: Hearings before the Subcommittee on Multinational Corporations,* 93rd Congress, 2nd session, 1974, part 7, pp. 46–50.
7. *CBS Evening News,* November 12, 1979.
8. *Washington Post,* November 13, 1979, p. 2.
9. *Mon centre cède, ma droite recule, situation excellente, j'attaque.*
10. *Time,* November 12, 1979, pp. 40–41. Ironically, Mobil's director of advertising, who designed the ad, resigned his position to become advertising director for Senator Ted Kennedy's presidential campaign. Kennedy is the number-one opponent of the oil industry. "The wolf also shall dwell with the lamb," Isaiah 11:1.
11. *Washington Post* owns *Newsweek* and television stations.
12. Irving Kristol, "Corporate Capitalism in America," *The Public Interest,* vol. 41, no. 124, pp. 133–35.
13. *Time,* August 27, 1979, pp. 24–33.
14. Martin C. Schnitzer, *Contemporary Government and Business Relations* (Chicago: Rand McNally, 1978), pp. 499–500.
15. "$159,000 to Teach Mothers How to Play with Their Babies," *Industry Week,* August 2, 1976, p. 1.

16. Senator Proxmire was recently sued by a professor who objected to winning the Golden Fleece Award.

17. *Time*, February 21, 1977, pp. 53–56.

18. The business advocacy role is supported by a recent Supreme Court decision, First National Bank of Boston v. Belotte, April 1978, which allows business firms to spend money to influence ballot decisions that do not materially affect business decisions.

19. An award-winning program that provides basic information about the levels and processes of government is being used by Dow Chemical to educate thousands of employees. This program, "It's Your Government, Too!" includes both video and written materials, and was conceived and written by Harrison Fox.

20. *Annual Report of General Motors: 1976*, p. 7.

21. "UMW Aids Consumer Bills in Pennsylvania Legislature," *United Mine Workers Journal*, August 1–15, 1975, p. 4.

22. "Scale-up Political Involvement, Urges NAM," *Industry Week*, October 14, 1974, p. 46.

23. "Get More Involved, Business Leaders Are Urged," *NAM Reports*, August 1976, p. 11.

24. "Becoming Directly Involved in Democracy," *Boise Cascade Quarterly*, August 1976, p. 11.

25. "Dear Alcoa Shareholders," *Alcoa News*, August 26, 1975.

26. "News Briefs," *Union Carbide Stockholders Quarterly*, May 1976, p. 1.

27. "Private Enterprise Versus Government Efficiency," *Happy Motoring News* (Exxon), vol. 15, September 1976.

28. "Public Policy Forums," American Enterprise Institute for Public Policy Research, Washington D.C.

29. See, for example, Robert B. Helms, *Natural Gas Regulation: An Evaluation of FPC Price Controls;* Paul W. MacAvoy and Robert S. Pindych, *Price Controls and the Natural Gas Shortage;* and Manuel F. Cohen and George Stigler, *Can Regulatory Agencies Protect the Consumer?*

30. See, for example, George W. Douglas and James C. Miller, *Economic Regulation of Domestic Air Transportation: Theory and Policy;* Roger C. Noll, *Reforming Regulation: An Evaluation of the Ash Council Proposals;* and Almarin Phillips, ed., *Promoting Competition in Regulated Markets.*

31. Congressional Assistantship Program Description," The Conference Board, February 1977.

32. U.S. Congress, Joint Economic Committee, *The 1979 Economic Report of the President,* February 1979.

33. U.S. Congress, Joint Economic Committee, *The 1979 Midyear Review of the Economy,* July 1979.

34. Donald B. Rice, "The Potentialities of Public Policy Research," *The Business-Government Relationship: A Reassessment,* Neil H. Jacoby, ed. (Pacific Palisades, Calif.: Goodyear Publishing Co., 1975).

35. Speech to the Society of American Newspaper Editors, January 17, 1925.

36. The former president of General Motors, Charles Wilson, once said, "What's good for General Motors is good for the country."

Chapter 5. Managing the Government Relations Function (pp. 55–67)

1. Statement by Reginald Jones appeared in *Congressional Quarterly,* September 17, 1977, p. 1968.

2. Ralph K. Winter, *Government and the Corporation* (Washington, D.C.: American Enterprise Institute, 1978), p. 66.

3. Harrison W. Fox, Jr., and Martin Schnitzer, "Managing the Government Relations Function," paper presented at the annual meeting of the Midwestern Business Administration Association, Chicago, April 1978; also Phyllis S. McGrath, *Managing Corporate External Relations* (New York: The Conference Board, 1976).

4. Robert W. Miller and Jimmy D. Johnson, *Corporate Ambassadors to Washington* (Washington: The American University, Center for the Study of Private Enterprise, 1970).

5. Harrison W. Fox, Jr., "It's Your Government, Too!" visual presentation written for Dow Chemical.

6. Howard L. Edwards, "Grass Roots Politics and Political Action Committees," *Mining Congress Journal,* May 1977, p. 38.

7. Emerging corporate-government issues have been studied by Robert Moore, who is emerging issues systems coordinator of the Conference Board. See Robert Moore, "Spotting Emergency Issues," paper presented at the conference held by the Public Relations Society of America, Washington, May 1978.

8. A small pizza shop may buy spices shipped directly from another state, and a farmer's decision to raise wheat in excess of government quotas and consume it on the farm is in reality a decision not to buy wheat in the open market, which may affect its price in interstate commerce.

9. Actually, thirteen states had antitrust laws before the Sherman Act was passed in 1890.

Chapter 6. The Political System (pp. 68–83)

1. Enumerated powers are those delegated to the federal government by the Constitution—the right to regulate commerce, coin money, levy taxes, and so forth.
2. Marbury v. Madison, 1 Cranch 137 (1803).
3. "Pudd'nhead Wilson's New Calendar," Chapter 2, *Following the Equator*, vol. 1.
4. Syndicated newspaper article, June 28, 1931.
5. "Capital Hill's Growing Army of Bureaucrats," *U.S. News and World Report,* December 24, 1979, p. 52.
6. Ibid., p. 55.
7. This is particularly true of the House of Representatives; however, the turnover among senators is much higher. In 1978, almost one-third of all senators up for reelection were defeated.
8. The Institute for Social Research at the University of Michigan asks the question, "Do you feel that almost all of the people running the government are smart people, or do you think that quite a few of them don't seem to know what they are doing?" The percentage choosing the latter view has increased from 28 percent in 1964 to 54 percent in 1978.
9. Peter Woll, *American Bureaucracy* (New York: W. W. Norton, 1963), pp. 142–148.
10. Leon D. Epstein, "The Old States in a New System," *The New American Political System,* Anthony King, ed. (Washington: American Enterprise Institute, 1978), pp. 325–369.
11. *King Henry VI, Part II,* act 4, scene 2.
12. Carl A. Auerbach and Samuel Mermin, *The Legal Process* (San Francisco: Chandler Publishing Company, 1961).
13. *Business Week,* October 8, 1979, p. 5.
14. Martin Shapiro, "The Supreme Court: From Warren to Burger," in King, *New American Political System,* pp. 179–211.
15. See Nathan Glazer, "Towards an Imperial Judiciary," *The Public Interest,* Fall 1976; also Raoul Berger, *Government by Judiciary* (Cambridge, Mass.: Harvard University Press, 1977).

Chapter 7. How Laws Are Passed
(pp. 84–98)

1. "Get More Involved, Business Leaders Are Urged," *NAM Reports,* August 11, 1975, p. 1.
2. "To Set the Economy Right," *Time,* August 27, 1979, p. 36.
3. *An Act of Congress,* presented for public television in April 1979.
4. "Ladling the butter from different tubs,/Stubbs butters Freeman, Freeman butters Stubbs," Anonymous.
5. Much of the material in this chapter is based on *An Act of Congress* and Charles J. Zinn, *How Our Laws Are Made* (Washington: U.S. Government Printing Office, 1978).
6. U.S. Congress, House of Representatives, *Clean Air Act Amendments of 1977, Part 1: Hearings before the Subcommittee on Health and the Environment of the Committee on Interstate and Foreign Commerce,* 95th Congress, 1st session, April 18, 1977, p. 389.

Chapter 8. Dealing with Legislators
(pp. 99–114)

1. On major legislation that has significant backing, a committee or one of its subcommittees will hold hearings to receive opinions. It then meets to "mark-up" (discuss and revise) and vote on the bill.
2. *U.S. News and World Report,* December 24, 1979, p. 55.
3. Whirlpool Corporation, "Federal Legislative Briefing," March 17, 1975.
4. *Hamlet,* act 2, scene 2.
5. *Lady Windermere's Fan,* act 1.
6. "Conference Is Success: H.R. 7132 Passes House," *The Postal Supervisor,* October 1977, pp. 2–3.
7. The Kennedy-Rodino bill would overturn the Supreme Court's Illinois Brick decision, which limited triple damage suits to direct purchasers.
8. A wholesaler who buys from a manufacturer is a direct purchaser. All of the others in the chain of distribution are indirect purchasers. If a manufacturer engages in illegal price-fixing, only the wholesaler can sue for triple damages.

9. "Letter to a Friend," 1908, in *Mark Twain's Correspondence with Henry Huddleston Rogers, 1893–1909* (Berkeley: University of California Press, 1969).
10. Prepared statement by Frank P. Samford, Jr., chairman of the board, Liberty Life Insurance Company, Birmingham, Alabama. Hearings before the Senate Judiciary Subcommittee on Antitrust and Monopoly, March 16, 1979.
11. Industrial life insurance is specifically designed to meet the needs of funeral expenses. In 1978 more than half the people who died in Alabama had industrial insurance.
12. Life insurance premiums for some insurance companies may be paid directly to the agent on a monthly collection basis. This is called monthly debit insurance, and it is particularly popular in rural areas and among low-income groups.

Chapter 9. How to Deal with Congressional Staffs (pp. 115–127)

1. Cited in Harrison W. Fox, Jr., and Susan Webb Hammond, *Congressional Staffs* (New York: The Free Press, 1977), p. 1.
2. *Congressional Record,* September 8, 1976, p. 15432.
3. Fox and Hammond, *Congressional Staffs,* Table 3, p. 171.
4. "Congress's Bureaucrats," *U.S. News and World Report,* December 24, 1979, p. 52.
5. Ibid., p. 53.
6. An example is Carol Browning, who was the personal secretary to former senator William E. Brock of Tennessee, and who remained his personal secretary when he became chairman of the Republican National Committee.
7. Statement attributed to Speaker Thomas B. Reed of Maine.
8. Fox and Hammond, *Congressional Staffs,* p. 177.
9. Ibid., p. 175.
10. Nelson W. Polsby, "The Institutionalization of the House of Representatives," *American Political Science Review,* vol. 62, 1968, pp. 144–168.
11. An example is Dr. Jerry Waters, who was the administrative assistant to former senator James Pearson of Kansas. When Senator Pearson retired, Waters was hired by a Washington lobbying firm.

Chapter 10. Administrative Agencies
(pp. 128–141)

1. The Administrative Procedure Act was passed in 1946 to establish more uniform hearing procedures among administrative agencies. It also expanded the scope of judicial review.
2. Munn v. Illinois (1877) justified public regulation on the basis that private property affected with a public interest ceases to be private.
3. Nebbia v. New York, 291 U.S. 502 (1934).
4. Alexander Hamilton, James Madison, and John Jay, *The Federalist* (New York: Tudor Publishing Co., 1937), p. 15.
5. The term *common law* refers to legal principles and practices made by judges that have characterized the Anglo-Saxon legal system.

Chapter 11. The Major Regulatory Agencies
(pp. 142–155)

1. U.S. Congress, Joint Economic Committee, *Hearings on the 1979 Economic Report of the President,* 1979, p. 32.
2. "The Costs of Government Regulation of Business," study prepared for the Subcommittee on Economic Growth and Stabilization, 1978.
3. The FTC has jurisdiction over Section 2 of the Clayton Act, which deals with what is called "primary-line" price discrimination, and over the Robinson-Patman Act, which amended Section 2 to prohibit "secondary-line" price discrimination. This refers to the sale of the same good to different buyers in the same geographic area at different prices when there is no cost difference.
4. Murray L. Weidenbaum, *Government-Mandated Price Increases* (Washington: American Enterprise Institute, 1975), p. 31.
5. Ibid., p. 38.
6. See the statement of John A. Busterud in *The Economic Impact of Environmental Regulations: Hearings before the Joint Economic Committee,* 93rd Congress, 2nd session, November 1974, pp. 127–132.
7. Chase Econometric Associates, *The Macroeconomic Impact of Federal Pollution Control Programs: 1976 Assessment,* report prepared for the Council on Environmental Quality, 1976, pp. 2–3.
8. *U.S. News and World Report,* February 11, 1980, pp. 78–84.
9. Arthur Anderson and Company, *Cost of Government Regulation*

Study for the Business Roundtable (New York: The Business Roundtable, 1979), p. 19.

10. Ibid., p. 22.
11. See U.S. District Court, Eastern District of Pennsylvania, Civil Action No. 73-149, Consent Decree, 1973.
12. Diane Crothers, "The AT&T Settlement," *Women's Rights Law Reporter,* vol. 1, no. 5, Summer 1973, pp. 8–12.
13. The above-mentioned Arthur Anderson and Company study mentions that the forty-eight participating companies had to complete more than three million pages of information in 1977 in order to supply and maintain records that provide proof of compliance.
14. Robert Stewart Smith, *Occupational Safety and Health Act* (Washington: American Enterprise Institute, 1976).
15. *Occupational Safety and Health Act,* Section 5a.
16. U.S. Congress, Senate, Committee on Labor and Public Welfare, *Legislative History of the Occupational Safety and Health Act of 1970,* 92nd Congress, 1st session, 1971.
17. Lewis Carroll, *Alice's Adventures in Wonderland and Through the Looking Glass* (New York: Airmont Publishing Co., 1965), p. 198.
18. *U.S. Code of Federal Regulations,* Title 29, Section 1910.25(b) (3) (ii).
19. Smith, *Occupational Safety and Health Act,* p. 1.
20. Ibid., p. 12.
21. U.S. Congress, Joint Economic Committee, *Government Regulation: America's Number One Growth Industry: Notes from the Joint Economic Committee,* vol. 4, number 11, May 16, 1978, p. 7.
22. "U.S. Will Clarify Statute on Corrupt Acts by American Firms Operating Overseas," *Wall Street Journal,* September 21, 1979, p. 20.
23. Sam Peltzman, *Regulation of Pharmaceutical Innovation: The 1962 Amendments* (Washington: American Enterprise Institute, 1974).
24. The Federal Energy Regulation Commission is an independent five-member commission within the Department of Energy. It has retained many of the functions of the Federal Power Commission, which it replaced when the Department of Energy was created, such as the setting of rates and charges for the transportation and sale of natural gas and for the transmission and sale of electricity and the licensing of hydroelectric power projects.
25. "Costs of Government Regulation of Business."
26. Gerald R. Rosen, "We're Going for Companies' Throats," *Dunn's Review,* January 1973, p. 36.

27. U.S. Congress, Joint Economic Committee, *Regulatory Budgeting and the Need for Cost-Effectiveness in the Regulatory Process,* 96th Congress, 1st session, August 1979, pp. 15–22.

Chapter 12. Dealing with Regulatory Agencies (pp. 156–167)

1. Lewis Carroll, *Alice's Adventures in Wonderland and Through the Looking Glass* (New York: Airmont Publishing Co., 1965), p. 166.
2. *U.S. News and World Report,* February 11, 1980, p. 78.
3. Karen Abarbanel, "New Era of Environmental Politics," *Reporter,* December 1977, p. 3.
4. U.S. Congress, Joint Economic Committee, *Environment Regulation: America's Number One Growth Industry: Notes from the Joint Economic Committee,* vol. 10, no. 11, May 16, 1978, p. 4.
5. See, for example, U.S. Senate, *Senate Report 1365,* 91st Congress, 2nd session.
6. Comptroller General of the United States, *Banning of Two Toys and Certain Aerosol Spray Adhesives,* MWD-75-65 (Washington: U.S. General Accounting Office, 1975), pp. 4–12.
7. Martin C. Schnitzer, *Contemporary Government and Business Relations* (Chicago: Rand McNally, 1978), pp. 389–390.
8. Ibid., p. 390.
9. Information provided by the former owner of the Marlin Toy Company.
10. Arthur M. Lewis, "Lessons from the Firestone Fracas," *Fortune,* August 28, 1978, p. 46.
11. Ibid., p. 47.
12. "The Impact of Government Regulation on the Dow Chemical Company," (Midland, Michigan: Dow Chemical).
13. Quoted in Aaron Wildavsky, *The Politics of the Budgetary Process,* 2nd ed. (Boston: Little, Brown, 1974), pp. 80–81.
14. Peter Woll, *American Bureaucracy* (New York: W. W. Norton, 1963), pp. 124–29.

Chapter 13. Lobbying: Is It a Dirty Word? (pp. 168–182)

1. Jack Anderson, "Lobbyists: The Unelected Lawmakers in Washington," *Parade,* March 16, 1980, pp. 4–6.
2. "The Nashville Advocate," WCDN-TV, Channel 8, March 18, 1974. Press release April 4, 1974.

3. Bryce Harlow, special assistant to President Eisenhower, displayed this sign in his office: Have you come up with the solution or are you part of the problem?

4. Steve Hess, "The Greatest Power Broker of His Era," *Capitol Hill,* Winter 1980, pp. 4–5.

5. Marrines S. Eccles, *Beckoning Frontiers,* Sidney Hyman, ed. (New York: Alfred A. Knopf, 1951), p. 336.

6. Barry M. Hager, "Carter Seeks More Effective Use of Departmental Lobbyists' Skills," *Congressional Quarterly,* March 4, 1978, p. 579.

7. U.S. Code, Title 18, sec. 1913. "No part of the money appropriated by any enactment of Congress shall, in the absence of express authorization by Congress, be used directly or indirectly to pay for any personal service, advertisement, telegram, telephone, letter, printed or written matter, or other device, intended or designed to influence in any manner a member of Congress, to favor or oppose, by vote or otherwise, any legislation or appropriation by Congress, whether before or after the introduction of any bill or resolution proposing such legislation or appropriation."

8. Spencer Rich, "White House Agencies Lobby Heavily on Hill," *Washington Post,* May 12, 1974, p. 15.

9. Donald H. Haider, *When Governments Come to Washington* (New York: The Free Press, 1974), pp. 32–40.

10. Bill Timmons was originally an administrative assistant to former congressman (later senator) William E. Brock of Tennessee. He now heads his own lobbying firm and is known as the "Rainmaker" because of his ability to change the weather on Capitol Hill.

11. Rich, "White House Agencies," p. 15.

12. Hager, "Carter Seeks More Effective Use," p. 581.

13. Ibid., p. 581.

14. Henry Louis Mencken, *Notes on Democracy* (New York: Octagon Books, 1977).

Chapter 14. Going to the Bank: Personalities and Debts (pp. 183–192)

1. David F. Pike, "Washington Lawyers: Rise of the Power Brokers," *U.S. News and World Report,* March 10, 1980, p. 56.

2. John T. Dunlop, Alfred D. Chandler, Jr., George P. Schultz, and

Irving S. Shapiro, "Business and Public Policy," *Harvard Business Review,* November-December 1979, p. 87.

3. Ibid., p. 100.

4. Pike, "Washington Lawyers," p. 53.

5. *Congressional Directory,* 96th Congress, 1st session (Washington: U.S. Government Printing Office, 1979), pp. 75–78.

6. James MacGregor Burns, J. W. Peltason, and Thomas E. Cronin, *Government by the People* (Englewood Cliffs, N.J.: Prentice-Hall, 1978), p. 253.

7. Episcopalians in Congress have a disproportionate relationship to the number of Episcopalians in society as a whole—15 percent compared with 1.5 percent.

8. John Cobbs, "Egalitarianism: The Corporation as Villain," *Business Week,* December 15, 1975, pp. 86–88.

9. Friedrich Hayek, *The Road to Serfdom* (Chicago: University of Chicago Press, 1944).

10. Amitai Etzioni, "Is the U.S. about to Become a Siesta Society?" *U.S. News and World Report,* April 14, 1980, p. 54.

Chapter 15. A Final Perspective on Business-Government Relations (pp. 193–203)

1. Lewis Carroll, *Alice's Adventures in Wonderland and Through the Looking Glass* (New York: Airmont Publishing Co., 1965), p. 124.

2. *Time,* April 7, 1980, p. 59.

3. Steven N. Brenner, "Business and Politics: An Update," *Harvard Business Review,* November-December 1979, pp. 162–163.

4. Ibid., p. 157.

5. Ibid., p. 155.

6. Edward Bellamy, *Looking Backward* (New York: The New American Library of World Literature, 1963).

7. "The Shrinking Standard of Living," *Business Week,* January 28, 1980, pp. 72–78.

8. *Candide,* chap. 1.

9. "U.S. Autos: Losing a Big Segment of the Market Forever?" *Business Week,* March 24, 1980, pp. 78–88.

Recommended
Readings

Recommended Readings

Chapter 1. The Political Marketplace

HABERLER, GOTTFRIED. *Challenge to a Free Market Economy*. Washington: American Enterprise Institute for Public Policy Research, 1975.

JACOBY, NEIL, ed. *The Business-Government Relationship: A Reassessment*. Pacific Palisades, Calif.: Goodyear, 1974.

SCHNITZER, MARTIN C. *Contemporary Government and Business Relations*. Chap. 1. Chicago: Rand McNally, 1978.

STIGLER, GEORGE. *The Citizen and the State*. Chicago: University of Chicago Press, 1975.

U.S. CONGRESS, JOINT ECONOMIC COMMITTEE. *Productivity in the Federal Government*, May 31, 1979.

WEIDENBAUM, MURRAY. *Business, Government, and the Public*. Englewood Cliffs, N.J.: Prentice-Hall, 1976.

WILCOX, CLAIRE, and SHEPHERD, WILLIAM G. *Public Policies Toward Business*. 6th ed., chap. 1. Homewood, Ill.: Richard D. Irwin, 1979.

223

Chapter 2. The Cost of Regulation

CRANDALL, ROBERT W. *Curbing the Costs of Social Regulation.* Washington: The Brookings Institution, 1979.

PELZMAN, SAM. *Regulation of Automobile Safety.* Washington: American Enterprise Institute, 1975.

U.S. CONGRESS, JOINT COMMITTEE FOR ECONOMIC DEVELOPMENT. *Redefining Government's Role in the Market System.* New York, July 1979.

U.S. CONGRESS, JOINT ECONOMIC COMMITTEE, *The Costs of Government Regulation of Business,* 1978.

U.S. CONGRESS, JOINT ECONOMIC COMMITTEE, *Technology, Economic Growth, and International Competitiveness.* Report prepared for the Subcommittee on Economic Growth, 1975.

WINTER, RALPH. *Government and the Corporation.* Washington: American Enterprise Institute, 1978.

Chapter 3. The Second Managerial Revolution

ANDERSON, MARTIN. *The Federal Bulldozer.* New York: McGraw-Hill, 1967.

BARBER, RICHARD J. *The American Corporation.* New York: E. P. Dutton, 1970.

DEMSETZ, HAROLD. *The Market Concentration Doctrine.* Washington: American Enterprise Institute, 1973.

HARGREAVES, JOHN, and DAUMAN, JAN. *Business Survival and Social Change: A Practical Guide to Responsibility and Partnership.* New York: John Wiley, 1975.

JACOBY, NEIL, *Corporate Power and Social Responsibility.* New York: Macmillan, 1977.

LODGE, GEORGE. *The New American Ideology.* New York: Alfred A. Knopf, 1975.

McGEE, JOHN S. *In Defense of Industrial Concentration.* New York: Praeger, 1971.

NADER, RALPH. *Taming the Giant Corporations.* New York: W. W. Norton, 1976.

SCHWARTZ, DONALD E. "Towards New Corporate Goals: Coexistence with Society." *Georgetown Law Review,* vol. 57., 1971.

WINTER, RALPH. *Government and the Corporation.* Washington: American Enterprise Institute, 1978.

Chapter 4. Business as Advocate

AMERICAN ENTERPRISE INSTITUTE FORUMS. *Professors, Politicians, and Public Policy.* Washington: American Enterprise Institute, 1978.

BELL, DANIEL. *The Coming of Post-Industrial Society.* New York: Basic Books, 1976.

BORK, ROBERT H. *Capitalism and the Corporate Executive.* Washington: American Enterprise Institute, 1977.

EPSTEIN, EDWARD J. *Between Fact and Fiction.* New York: Random House, 1975.

HAYEK, FRIEDRICH. *The Road to Serfdom.* Chicago: University of Chicago Press, 1944.

KRISTOL, IRVING. *Two Cheers for Capitalism.* New York: Basic Books, 1978.

MOYNIHAN, DANIEL P. "Social Policy: From the Utilitarian Ethic to the Therapeutic Ethic," in *Qualities of Life,* Commission on Critical Choices. Lexington, Mass.: D. C. Heath, 1976.

SCHNITZER, MARTIN C. *Contemporary Government and Business Relations.* Chapter 17. Chicago: Rand McNally, 1978.

WINTER, RALPH. *Government and the Corporation.* Washington: American Enterprise Institute, 1978.

Chapter 5. Managing the Government Relations Function

EASTMAN, HOPE. *Lobbying: A Constitutionally Protected Right.* Washington: American Enterprise Institute, 1978.

LEONE, ROBERT. "The Real Costs of Regulation." *Harvard Business Review,* November-December, 1977.

McGRATH, PHYLLIS S. *Managing Corporate External Relations.* New York: The Conference Board, 1976.

MILLER, ROBERT W., and JOHNSON, JIMMY D. *Corporate Ambassadors to Washington.* Washington: American University, Center for the Study of Private Enterprise, 1970.

MOORE, ROBERT. "Spotting Emerging Issues." Paper presented at the Public Relations Society of America Annual Conference, Washington, May 9, 1978.

NOVAK, MICHAEL. *The American Vision: An Essay on the Future of Democratic Capitalism.* Washington: American Enterprise Institute, 1979.

O'TOOLE, JAMES. "What's Ahead for the Business-Government Relationship." *Harvard Business Review,* March-April 1979.

SEELYE, ALFRED L. "Societal Change and Business-Government Relationships." *MSU Business Topics,* Autumn, 1975, pp. 1–6.

WEIDENBAUM, MURRAY. *Business, Government, and the Public.* Englewood Cliffs, N.J.: Prentice-Hall, 1976.

Chapter 6. The Political System

BALZANO, MICHAEL. *Reorganizing the Federal Bureaucracy: The Rhetoric and the Reality.* Washington: American Enterprise Institute, 1978.

CASPER, JONATHAN. "The Supreme Court and National Policy Making." *American Political Science Review,* vol. 60, 1976, pp. 50–61.

DAHL, ROBERT. "Decision-Making in a Democracy: The Supreme Court as a National Policy Maker." *Journal of Public Law,* vol. 6, 1957, pp. 277–295.

FOX, HARRISON W., JR., and HAMMOND, SUSAN WEBB. *Congressional Staffs.* New York: The Free Press, 1977.

HECLO, HUGH. *A Government of Strangers.* Washington: The Brookings Institution, 1977.

JEWELL, MALCOLM E., and PATTERSON, SAMUEL C. *The Legislative Process in the United States.* 3rd ed. New York: Random House, 1977.

KING, ANTHONY, ed. *The New American Political System.* Washington: American Enterprise Institute, 1978.

ORNSTEIN, NORMAN J., *Congress in Change.* New York: Praeger, 1975.

RIPLEY, RANDALL B. *Congress: Process and Policy.* New York: W. W. Norton, 1975.

WOLL, PETER. *American Bureaucracy.* New York: W. W. Norton, 1963.

Chapter 7. How Laws Are Passed

ASBELL, BERNARD. *The Senate Nobody Knows.* New York: Doubleday, 1978.

BARONE, MICHAEL, et. al. *The Almanac of American Politics.* New York: Dutton, 1978.

DODD, LAURENCE, and OPPENHEIMER, BRUCE. *Congress Reconsidered.* New York: Praeger, 1977.

FIORINA, MORRIS. *Congress: Keystone of the Washington Establishment.* New Haven: Yale University Press, 1977.

Jones, Charles O. *Clean Air: The Policies and Politics of Pollution Control.* Pittsburgh: University of Pittsburgh Press, 1975.

Peabody, Robert L. *Leadership in Congress.* Boston: Little, Brown, 1977.

Redman, Eric. *The Dance of Legislation.* New York: Simon and Schuster, 1973.

Zinn, Charles J. *How Our Laws Are Made.* Washington: U.S. Government Printing Office, 1978.

Chapter 8. Dealing with Legislators

Barone, Michael, et. al. *The Almanac of American Politics.* New York: Dutton, 1978.

Clapp, Charles L. *The Congressman: His Work As He Sees It.* Washington: The Brookings Institution, 1973.

Congressional Directory. Washington: U.S. Government Printing Office, 1979.

Congressional Guide to the U.S. Congress. Washington: Congressional Quarterly Service, 1979.

Fenno, Richard F. *Homestyle: Congressmen in Their Constituencies.* Boston: Little, Brown, 1978.

Mayhew, David. *Congress: The Electoral Connection.* New Haven: Yale University Press, 1974.

Oleszek, Walter. *Congressional Procedures and the Policy Process.* Washington: Congressional Quarterly Service, 1978.

Ornstein, Norman J., and Elder, Shirley. *Interest Groups, Lobbying, and Policy Making.* Washington: Congressional Quarterly Service, 1978.

Polsby, Nelson W. *Congress and the Presidency.* Englewood Cliffs, N.J.: Prentice-Hall, 1975.

Udall, Morris K. *The Job of the Congressman.* New York: Bobbs-Merrill, 1970.

Chapter 9. How to Deal with Congressional Staffs

Davidson, Roger. *The Role of the Congressman.* New York: Pegasus, 1969.

Fiorina, Morris. *Congress: Keystone of the Washington Establishment.* New Haven: Yale University Press, 1977.

FOX, HARRISON W., JR., and HAMMOND, SUSAN WEBB. *Congressional Staffs.* New York: The Free Press, 1977.

GRIFFITH, ERNEST S., and VALEO, FRANCIS. *Congress: Its Contemporary Role.* New York: New York University Press, 1975.

KOFMEHL, KENNETH. *Professional Staffs of Congress.* West Lafayette, Indiana: Purdue University Press, 1977.

OLESZEK, WALTER. *Congressional Procedures and the Policy Process.* Washington: Congressional Quarterly Service, 1978.

PEABODY, ROBERT, and POLSBY, NELSON. *New Perspectives on the House of Representatives.* 3rd ed. Chicago: Rand McNally, 1977.

RIPLEY, RANDALL B. *Congress: Process and Policy.* New York: W. W. Norton, 1975.

SALOMA, JOHN S. *Congress and the New Politics.* Boston: Little, Brown, 1972.

WILSON, JAMES O. *Political Organizations.* New York: Basic Books, 1973.

Chapter 10. Administrative Agencies

ANDERSON, JAMES E., ed. *Economic Regulatory Policies.* Carbondale, Ill.: Southern Illinois Press, 1976.

ASH, ROY L. *The Political World, Government Regulation, and Spending.* Los Angeles, Calif.: International Institute for Economic Research, 1979.

CRAFTON, CARL. "The Creation of Federal Agencies." *Administration and Society,* November 1975, pp. 328–365.

GREENWALD, CAROL. *Group Power Lobbying and Public Policy.* New York: Praeger, 1977.

LILLY, WILLIAM, and MILLER, JAMES. "The New Social Regulation." *The Public Interest,* Spring 1977.

ROURKE, FRANCES E. *Bureaucracy, Politics and Public Policy.* 2nd ed. Boston: Little, Brown, 1976.

WALTERS, ALAN A. *The Politization of Economic Decisions.* Los Angeles, Calif.: International Institute for Economic Research, 1976.

WHITAKER, JOHN C. *Striking a Balance.* Washington: American Enterprise Institute; Palo Alto, Calif: Hoover Institution, 1976.

WILSON, JAMES O. "The Dead Hand of Regulation." *The Public Interest,* Fall 1971.

WOLL, PETER. *American Bureaucracy.* New York: W. W. Norton, 1963.

Chapter 11. The Major Regulatory Agencies

ALLEWELT, WILLIAM F. *Bureaucratic Intervention, Economic Efficiency, and the Free Society: An Episode.* Los Angeles: International Institute for Economic Research, May 1977.

ARTHUR ANDERSON AND CO. *Cost of Government Regulation Study for the Business Roundtable.* New York: The Business Roundtable, March 1979.

DEMSETZ, HAROLD. *The Trust behind Antitrust.* Los Angeles: International Institute for Economic Research, March 1978.

GRABOWSKI, HENRY G. *Drug Regulation and Innovation.* Washington: American Enterprise Institute, 1976.

MACAVOY, PAUL W. *The Regulated Industries and the Economy.* New York: W. W. Norton, 1979.

PHILLIPS, ALMARIN, ed. *Promoting Competition in Regulated Industries.* Washington: The Brookings Institution, 1975.

STEWART, ROBERT S. *The Occupational Safety and Health Act.* Washington: American Enterprise Institute, 1976.

U.S. CONGRESS, HOUSE OF REPRESENTATIVES, SUBCOMMITTEE ON SPECIAL SMALL BUSINESS PROBLEMS. *Regulatory Problems of the Independent Owner-Operator in the Nation's Trucking Industry.* 95th Congress, 2nd session, 1978.

U.S. CONGRESS, JOINT ECONOMIC COMMITTEE, *Regulatory Budgeting and the Need for Cost-Effectiveness in the Regulatory Process.* 96th Congress, 1st session, 1979.

Chapter 12. Dealing with Regulatory Agencies

CATER, DOUGLASS. *Power in Washington.* New York: Random House, 1964.

DOWNS, ANTHONY. *Inside Bureaucracy.* Boston: Little, Brown, 1967.

FREEMAN, J. LEIPER. *The Political Process.* Rev. ed. New York: Doubleday, 1965.

GREENWALD, CAROL. *Group Power Lobbying and Public Policy.* New York: Praeger, 1977.

HEILO, HUGH. *A Government of Strangers: Executive Politics in Washington.* Washington: The Brookings Institution, 1977.

KAUFMAN, HERBERT. *Are Government Organizations Immortal?* Washington: The Brookings Institution, 1976.

ROURKE, FRANCES E. *Bureaucracy, Politics and Public Policy.* 2nd ed. Boston: Little, Brown, 1976.

WILDAVSKY, AARON. *The Politics of the Budgetary Process.* 2nd ed. Boston: Little, Brown, 1974.

Chapter 13. Lobbying: Is It a Dirty Word?

BLAISDELL, DONALD. *American Democracy Under Pressure.* New York: Ronald Press, 1957.

CONGRESSIONAL QUARTERLY SERVICE. *Legislators and the Lobbyists.* 2nd ed. Washington, 1978.

DEAKIN, JAMES. *The Lobbyists.* Washington: Public Affairs Press, 1966.

DEXTER, LOUIS. *How Organizations Are Represented in Washington.* Indianapolis: Bobbs-Merrill, 1969.

ELAZAR, DANIEL J. *The American Partnership.* Chicago: University of Chicago Press, 1962.

HAIDER, DONALD H. *When Governments Come to Washington.* New York: The Free Press, 1974.

HOLTZMAN, ABRAHAM. *Interest Groups and Lobbying.* New York: Macmillan, 1968.

NEUSTADT, RICHARD E. *Presidential Power.* New York: John Wiley, 1976.

RUDER, WILLIAM, and NATHAN, RAYMOND. *The Businessman's Guide to Washington.* New York: Macmillan, 1975.

TRUMAN, DAVID B. *The Governmental Process: Political Interests and Public Opinion.* 2nd ed. New York: Alfred A. Knopf, 1971.

Chapter 14. Going to the Bank: Personalities and Debts

CLAPP, CHARLES L. *The Congressman: His Work As He Sees It.* Washington: The Brookings Institution, 1973.

CLAUSEN, AAGE R. *How Congressmen Decide.* New York: St. Martin's, 1973.

DAVIDSON, ROGER. *The Role of the Congressman.* New York: Pegasus, 1969.

DUNLOP, JOHN T., CHANDLER, ALFRED D., SCHULTZ, CHARLES P., and SHAPIRO, IRVING S. "Business and Public Policy." *Harvard Business Review,* November-December 1979, pp. 85–102.

FIORINA, MORRIS P. *Congress: Keystone of the Washington Establishment.* New Haven: Yale University Press, 1977.

MATTHEWS, DONALD R. *The Social Background of Political Decision-Makers.* New York: Doubleday, 1954.

RHODES, JOHN J. *The Futile System.* Washington: EPM Publications, 1976.

SUMMER, CHARLES E. *Strategic Behavior in Business and Government.* Boston: Little, Brown, 1980.

Chapter 15. A Final Perspective on Business-Government Relations

BAUER, RAYMOND A. *American Business and Public Policy: The Politics of Foreign Trade.* Chicago: Aldine, 1979.

BRENNER, STEVEN N. "Business and Politics: An Update." *Harvard Business Review,* November-December 1979, pp. 149–163.

DREW, ELIZABETH. *The Senator.* New York: Simon and Schuster, 1979.

FENN, DAN H. "Finding Where the Power Lies in Government." *Harvard Business Review,* September-October 1979, pp. 144–153.

FLEMING, JOHN E. "The Future of U.S. Government-Corporate Relations." *Long Range Planning,* vol. 12, August 1979, pp. 20–26.

KRAAR, LOUIS. "The Multinationals Get Smarter about Political Risks." *Fortune,* March 1980, pp. 86–100.

TODD, JERRY C. "A Model for Valuation of Managerial Resources." *CLU Journal,* January 1980, pp. 26–33.

WEIDENBAUM, MURRAY L. *The Future of Business Regulation.* New York: AMACON, 1979.

Index

Index